Chosen

A BIBLICAL LOOK AT WHY ISRAEL WAS CHOSEN AND
WHAT THAT HAS TO DO WITH THE CHURCH TODAY

NICOLE PARKS

© 2024 by Nicole Parks. Written by Nicole Parks.
Cover water color by Chesed Anne Dent Fitzsimons (ChesedCo Maps).
Cover layout and interior layout designed by 3C Expressions, Inc.

All Scripture quotations, unless otherwise indicated, are taken from The Holy Bible, New International Version (NIV). © 1973, 1978, 1984, 2011 by Biblica, Inc. TM Used by permission. All rights reserved worldwide.

All rights reserved. No part of this publication may be reproduced, stored in a retrieval system, or transmitted in any form or by any means—electronic, mechanical, photocopying, recording, or otherwise—without prior written permission.

IBSN: 978-0-9987677-2-7

TO QUOTE THE MUSICIAN CHARLIE HALL,
THIS BOOK IS DEDICATED TO "THE CHILDREN WHO
SLEEP BENEATH CITIES AT DARK. LET LOVE COME AND
TOUCH THEM WITH YOUR FATHER'S HEART."

Table of Contents

INTRODUCTION	1
IN THE BEGINNING	6
Creation	6
The Fall	7
The Decline	9
THE COVENANT	12
The Abrahamic Covenant	12
The Sons of Abram	17
The Patriarchs	22
The Sons of Israel	28
THE CHOSEN PEOPLE	30
The Exodus	30
Chosen	35
The Promised Land	37
The Law	39
The Tabernacle	42
THE JOURNEY	44
Leviticus	44
Wandering	47
Homecoming	49
Strong and Courageous	54
The Period of the Judges	56
SUMMARY	58
UNDERSTANDING THE HISTORICAL ARRANGEMENT IN THE OT	60
THE HISTORY	63
Samuel, the Prophet Priest	63
Saul, the People's King	65
David, the Shepherd King	67
Solomon, the Wise King	71
Divided	77
Exile	78

PROPHECY	82
Pending Judgment	82
A Prophesied Messiah	84
Jeremiah, the Weeping Prophet	88
Ezekiel and Jonah	90
Isaiah	93
Great Distress	96
INTRODUCTION TO THE NEW TESTAMENT	98
THE MESSIAH	100
The Coming of the Messiah	100
The Ministry of Jesus	103
One: Jesus the Israelite	104
Jesus the Israelite Calls His Own	109
Two: Jesus for All	111
Three: The Kingdom has Come	115
Four: Authority to Go	118
Five: Death and Resurrection	121
THE NEW COVENANT	125
The Jew of Jews	125
Fatherhood and Adoption	130
Purchased	131
APPLICATION FOR TODAY	135
Modern Day Israel and the Covenant	135
Jerusalem	140
The Church and Israel	144
CONCLUSION	148
APPENDIX 1 - END TIMES PROPHECY	151
ACKNOWLEDGMENTS	155
BIBLIOGRAPHY	157
SCRIPTURE INDEX	160
ABOUT THE AUTHOR	168

Introduction

On Saturday October 7, 2023, Hamas launched a surprise attack from Gaza into Israel, killing many civilians and sparking yet another heated international debate surrounding the history of the Israeli-Palestinian conflict. The conflict, though less than a century old, is one of the most complicated and nuanced conflicts in recent history. I have read, studied, learned, and wrestled with my own internal conflict surrounding this topic since I was first exposed to it in early 2014. The writing of this book is the product of that decade-long soul wrestling.

In 2014, I had an opportunity to go and visit Israel and Palestine. As our trip leader was giving vision for the trip, he reminded us that we were going to walk on the very same dirt that Jesus had walked on. We would minister in cities where Jesus ministered 2,000 years ago. My husband and I served on a humanitarian aid trip meant to help Palestinian Muslims on the West Bank experience the love of Christ. That trip changed the trajectory of my life. I fell in love with the culture and the people like I had not ever experienced before, nor have I experienced anywhere else since. Despite that, I wrestled with a deep sadness. As a Christian, my life has been transformed by the power and presence of Jesus Christ. I have joy and hope and peace that exists only because of that decision to make Jesus the Lord of my life. I met many Palestinian Muslims who live without hope or peace.

I also met many Israeli Jews who lacked the joy and peace that I experience in my relationship with Jesus. I witnessed on numerous occasions a striving to keep the law that seemed to be almost a moving target. I'll never forget the first time I was introduced to a shabbat elevator. One of the hotels that we stayed at in Galilee had one and our host explained how it worked. He said that on shabbat, or the day of sabbath, no one was allowed to do any work at all. Producing a spark of electricity was considered "work" for some devout Jews. In this case, pushing the elevator button might be considered "work" by those holding to the letter of the law devoutly. Therefore, there existed an elevator that would take everyone to the very top floor and then automatically stop at each floor on the way down without the need for anyone to push a button. Although we had a bit of a chuckle over this entirely foreign concept, I began wondering where this thought process ends. For a chronic over-thinker *and* rule-follower such as myself, I would make myself crazy trying to keep the law. If merely pushing a button might be considered work, what could you do at all besides lay still on a couch and pray that over-thinking is not considered work?

I found myself wondering where the freedom and joy in the two opposing belief systems was that I encountered. In Islam, the hope is that your good deeds balance out the bad deeds enough to merit a favorable afterlife. In modern Judaism, the hope is that because of your ethnicity you are saved, but there are still hundreds of laws to keep in order to be sure of that. I went back to the Holy Lands three more times, year after year, and fell more in love each time. However, with each visit, I would learn more about the history of the people, the land, and the conflict therein. Every time I learned more, I somehow felt like I knew less.

I read books and articles trying to understand the conflict. I wanted to gain an accurate understanding of it, but it seemed like everything I read was very biased towards one side or the other. Furthermore, so many arguments on both sides seemed to make sense. Israel had been given the land by God, but then they lost it, also by God's sovereignty. Palestinians had been in the land for centuries. Obviously, the Jewish people needed a safe haven after the Holocaust. It made sense for that safe haven to be in the land of their ancestors, but what of the current occupants? The history was so complicated. And yet, my heart grieved for the people in that conflicted land.

That brings us to today, or rather the second week of October 2023. After the Hamas attack, Israel retaliated in full force. Innocent lives were lost on both sides.

Civilians, women, children. It has been as devastating as it has been divisive. On one side of the proverbial coin is the pro-Israel/anti-terrorist voice screaming for justice and demanding that the world stands with Israel. These voices are predominantly the Christians, the Americans, the Zionists, and the Jewish people. Personally, I am an American Christian. But I have not found a home for my voice in this group. Knowing from personal experience that the majority of Palestinians do not side with Hamas or any form of terrorism, my heart ached for the innocent Palestinians.

On the other side of the proverbial coin is the pro-Palestine/anti-oppressor voice, also screaming for justice and demanding freedom for Palestine from Israeli occupation. These voices would call themselves the humanitarians, those fighting for those who cannot fight for themselves. Many are Muslim, but certainly not all. They are decisively anti-Israel and for that reason, I have not found a home for my voice here either. It seemed that my voice could not find a home on either side of a debate that was so decisively against the other.

On the night of October 14, 2023, I found myself in tears sharing my feelings with my husband. Although he had had the same personal encounters and experiences in Israel and Palestine, and although he has a deep love for the people, he did tend to side more with the necessity to stand with Israel and their right to defend themselves against Hamas. Despite our amazing marriage and wonderful relationship, I found myself afraid to say aloud what I was thinking. But I found my voice as I said, "I do not stand with Hamas and the atrocities they have and continue to commit. However, I also cannot stand with a nation committing war crimes, genocide, and ethnic cleansing because of what I believe to be a superstitious misinterpretation of Scripture." I wept for the lost sheep of Israel (Matt. 10:6). I also wept for the lost sons and daughters of Ishmael, the Palestinians. My sweet husband listened lovingly, not agreeing or disagreeing as I poured my heart out. I told him how alone I felt in my opinions and feelings, but also how strongly I felt that what I was feeling was more aligned with Scripture and the heart of God than most of what I had heard from either opposing side.

The next day, he spent an hour in his prayer closet and although I did not ask what he was praying about, I felt certain it was me. When seemingly every Christian we know, every prophet he listens to, every pastor he follows, and those who have Masters of Divinity and Doctorates of Ministry were saying with certainty and conviction that we must stand with Israel, how could I dare to say that I think they might be wrong? No doubt, he wondered if I was some sort of apostate or heretic. But if I am just being honest (which I almost always am and sometimes to a fault), I have wrestled with these thoughts for years. I know the Bible quite well. I have read it cover to cover multiple times. I went to seminary and graduated with a 4.0 GPA and Masters of Global Studies degree. I have written a Bible study that shows an overview of the whole Bible from Genesis to Revelation, highlighting God's heart for the nations and the biblical basis for global missions. I teach all over the southeast on that, as well as the grand narrative of Scripture and the Abrahamic Covenant. I do not say all this to toot my own horn, but rather to show that although I do not claim to be an expert, I do bring some level of expertise and experience to the topic, and I have done extensive study on it for the past ten years. However, after really vocalizing to my husband how I actually feel about the necessity of standing with Israel and briefly sharing my understanding of how the Scriptures have informed that opinion, I realized that I needed to do a deeper dive into this topic.

I truly believe that God has been leading me to write this for years and I have put off doing so out of fear. This opinion will not be welcomed in many evangelical circles, no matter how well-researched and biblically based it is. I have no doubt that some people will say that anything justifying not standing with Israel is antisemitic, though I hope to show that there is absolutely no basis for that accusation. My purpose in doing this research and writing it out is first and foremost out of obedience. I feel as though God has led me and equipped me to do this, despite years of trying to convince Him that I am not qualified. (Moses did the same thing so at least I was in good company.) He has repeatedly shown me that He is the one who makes us "worthy of his calling, and that by his power he may bring to fruition [our] every desire for goodness and [our] every deed prompted by faith" (2 Thess. 1:11). In other words, He does not call the worthy and equipped, He equips and makes worthy the called.

My second reason for finally taking on this project is because I truly believe that there is a huge misunderstanding of one of the most important parts of Scripture, that being the Abrahamic Covenant. The covenant that God made with Abraham in Genesis chapter twelve is one of my greatest biblical passions. It is the turning point of God's story, the thread woven throughout all of Scripture, and one of the most unifying themes in the entire Bible. I do not believe that we can fully understand the Old Testament, the nation of Israel, the coming of Jesus, the New Testament, and the cohesive story they all create without having an accurate understanding of the Abrahamic Covenant. Furthermore, if that is the lynchpin in the biblical justification for unconditionally standing with modern-day Israel, it needs to be understood fully. Therefore, a significant portion of this writing will be focused on that. Having an accurate understanding of that covenant is just as important to the Jew as it is to the Christian, yet historically both groups have lacked that understanding.

Finally, my intention in this writing is not to convince you whether or not to stand with Israel or Palestine. My hope is to show you that God cares equally for the Israeli Jew and the Palestinian Muslim, as well as the American Christian, the European atheist, the Thai Buddhist, the Indian Hindu, and every single other man, woman, and child on this planet who bears His image. We all carry His image, even though we do not all yet carry and reflect His glory. Jesus came because God loves the whole world (John 3:16), not just the parts of the world that we agree with politically or relate to culturally. Jesus purchased for God *with His blood* "members of every tribe and language and people and nation" (Rev. 5:9) and I firmly believe that He will not return until He gets all that He paid for (Matt. 24:14). This book will explore that.

My prayer is that you come to this reading with an open heart and an open mind, allowing God to speak to you through His word, the holy Scriptures. We know that "the word of God is alive and active. Sharper than any double-edged sword, it penetrates even to dividing soul and spirit, joints and marrow" (Heb. 4:12). My words do not carry the power and anointing to convict the heart of man, but His words do. As I have written this, I have prayed over and over that the words I pen are from Him. I have prayed that as I write, if there is anything in my mind or notes or intentions that is not from Him, that it would be erased. I only want what He has for us. However, my life is a testimony of my own personal fallibility, so I beseech you to take everything you read back to the Lord. Through His word and the discernment from the Holy Spirit, I know He will guide you into all truth (John 16:13). I pray that this writing serves as merely a tool for guiding you along the way.

In the Beginning

CREATION

In order to eventually get to the place where we can come to a mutual understanding of our responsibility in standing with modern-day Israel, we have to lay a very solid biblical foundation of who Israel is throughout the Scriptures. The only way to do that is to start at the very beginning of God's great story. Whether you are a Jew, Christian, Muslim, or even an atheist, you probably have at least a basic understanding of the Judeo-Christian beliefs about creation. However, given the sensitivity and significance of the topic at hand, I will try not to make assumptions about your knowledge and belief in elements of God's story that are critical for the topic.

In the beginning, God existed before anything and everything else. He simply was (Gen. 1:1). Through the power of His Spirit and His spoken Word, He created the heavens and the earth, the light and the dark, the waters of the seas, and the great lights of the sky. He filled His creation with life. The oceans teemed, the skies sang, and the hills and valleys roared with the sound of His creation. As beautiful as His creation was, it was not complete until He endowed it with His own image. God said, "Let us make human beings in our image, in our likeness, so that they may rule … over all the creatures" (Gen. 1:26). God created us, male and female, in His very own image (Gen. 1:27). Then He blessed His image-bearers and issued them His very first command in Genesis 1:28, saying, "Be fruitful and increase in number; fill the earth and subdue it." God's plan was to fill His creation with those who bore His image and reflected His glory.

Not only was the propagation of His image in all the earth important, but also the priority of relationship. Living in relationship with His creation was and is important to Him. Throughout the creation account in the first two chapters of Genesis, we see that after everything God created, He declared it good with only one exception. In Genesis 2:18, God indicated the only part of His creation that was lacking when He said, "It is *not good* for the man to be alone." Relationship with His creation and within His creation were of high priority because our God is a relational being. Finally, His creation was complete, and He called it "very good" (Gen. 1:31).

THE FALL

The third chapter of Genesis is the beginning of the undoing of God's good plan. His image in humanity was marred and the relationships were broken. Before the fall, Adam and Eve had everything they needed and wanted. They had a beautiful buffet of organic, vegan delicacies created by their Creator that could sustain and nourish them (Gen. 2:16). There was only one restriction, the forbidden fruit of the tree of the knowledge of good and evil. The warning God issued was that if they ate of it, they would certainly die (Gen. 2:17; 3:3). The fruit itself did not actually kill them, of course. In the words of the deceiver, if they ate of that particular tree, their "eyes [would] be opened, [they would] become like God, knowing good and evil" (Gen. 3:5). Another way of saying this is that they would insist upon determining in their own understanding and opinions what qualifies as good and what qualifies as evil.

Creator God, the loving designer and author of life, the One who walked with them in the garden "in the cool of the day" (Gen. 3:8), had insisted upon His right to define good and evil in His own terms. He created the game of life, therefore He got to make up the rules. As players often do, Adam and Eve decided to try out their own rules, seeking a shortcut to wisdom (Gen. 3:6) in order to be like God. With that decision came shame and brokenness of relationship. The relationship with God was marred, as evidenced from their decision to hide from their Father instead of running to Him (Gen. 3:10). The relationship between husband and wife was marred (Gen. 3:6), Eve's role as helper had been corrupted, and Adam cast blame not only on his bride, but on God for sending her (v. 12). As a result, the relationship between mankind and creation would also be marred. Neither the ground nor the womb would yield their harvest as effortlessly as God had designed (Gen. 3:16-19).

Mankind found themselves in a dire situation. Without an intentional look at the story, we might be tempted to view God as harsh or quick to anger. But let us quickly attempt to correct the marred image of the good Father through this story. Genesis chapter three, though one of the darkest days in history, shows the great mercy and love of God for those who have eyes to see it. He had given them everything and only had one rule. He had clearly communicated the consequences of breaking that one rule. Although the consequence was death, it did not come from the hand of God. It was merely the consequence of their sinful action. God's response to them was one of mercy. He sent them away *not from His presence* but from the tree of life. In verse twenty-two, God says, "The man has now become like one of us, knowing good and evil. He must not be allowed to reach out his hand and take also from the tree of life and eat, and live forever." God's mercy would not allow His children to live in an eternal state of sin and shame. How merciful is our God.

Furthermore, in verse twenty-one, we see another picture of His merciful goodness. It says, "The Lord God made garments of skin for Adam and his wife and clothed them." This is the very first sacrifice in Scripture. This is the very first death recorded in Scripture. Although we do not know if it was a cow or a sheep who gave up its life to clothe them, we know that some animal had to die in order for them to be clothed. A life was sacrificed to cover their shame. My guess is that it was a lamb. Probably spotless and blameless.

Lastly, in the midst of God explaining the consequences of their actions, He already foreshadowed that a day would come when good and evil would not have to be defined by human terms anymore because evil would be defeated once and for all. The deceiver, the enemy of mankind, would bruise the heel of man but one born of a woman would ultimately crush him. In all of history, there has only been one man born *only* of a woman. Adam and Eve were created by God Himself, no egg or sperm necessary. Every other human being throughout history has been born of egg (woman) and sperm (man). Except for one. Jesus of Nazareth, born of woman and Spirit. And when He came, He took the curse of mankind, the "thorns and thistles" produced by a cursed ground (Gen. 3:18), and He wore them as a crown as He crushed the head of the deceiver. In the midst of the fall, mankind may have marred everything good that God had created, but God was still good, loving His children with an everlasting, merciful, and redemptive love, telling them that one day He would undo what they had done.

THE DECLINE

The next few chapters in the book of Genesis show the decline of man after the fall. It is clearly shown that mankind's insistence on defining good and evil in their own terms simply did not go well for them. The first offshoots of God's image-bearers committed one of the most atrocious acts in the eyes of God. Cain, the firstborn of Adam and Eve, committed the first murder in history. In a fit of jealous rage, he killed his very own brother Abel (Gen. 4:6-8). At this point in God's story, there was no law or defined sin yet. But murder stood in direct opposition to God's first command from Genesis 1:28, where He told mankind to fill the earth with those who bore His image and reflected His glory. Additionally, since death itself is a direct consequence of the fall, murder would grieve the heart of God in ways we cannot imagine. God mourned for His fallen image-bearer as Abel's blood cried out to Him from the ground (Gen. 4:10).

God granted another son, Seth, to Adam and Eve, one through whom a line of righteousness would come. Adam bore the image of God and Seth bore the image of Adam (Gen. 5:3). Through the line of Adam and Seth, we can trace the righteousness of that original image of God through men like Enoch, who "walked faithfully with God" (Gen. 5:24) and Noah, "a righteous man, blameless among the people of his time" (Gen. 6:9). Almost 2,000 years had passed between Adam and Noah, and the wickedness of God's image-bearers became more than His Spirit would contend with (Gen. 6:3).

Despite the wickedness, God would not wipe His image from the earth entirely. Instead, He found among them one righteous man and his family, and He established a covenant with them (Gen. 6:18). Noah "in holy fear built an ark to save his family. By his faith he condemned the world and became heir of the righteousness that is in keeping with faith" (Heb. 11:7). Imagine the faith it takes to believe a flood would come despite the fact that at that point, God had never sent rain on the earth. Humans did not even have a concept in their minds for water coming from the sky because up to this point, it had only sprung up from the earth (Gen. 7:11).

For years, Noah built a boat in a land-locked place, no doubt enduring criticism and mocking. For forty days, rain poured throughout the earth, wiping away the wicked. For nearly a year, Noah and his family floated upon the instrument of God's judgment. Finally, after the waters dried up and the ark came to rest on dry ground, God once again simultaneously blessed and commanded His image-bearers to "be fruitful and increase in number and fill the earth" (Gen. 9:1).

An oft overlooked part of the flood story is in chapter nine. Think for a moment about actually cohabitating with two kinds of *every* animal on the planet. How did it not look like something out of National Geographic in that ark? Surely the lions would have devoured the gazelles and the bears would have mauled the humans. Yet, they all survived (Gen. 8:16-17). The fear and dread of man had not yet fallen on the animals. That is, until after the flood. God allowed for the killing of animals after the flood while simultaneously condemning the killing of humans. "You are no longer vegan," He said in verse 9:3. (Paraphrase mine.) But they were to live in a manner fitting image-bearers of the Creator (Gen. 9:4-5). Then He said, "Whoever sheds human blood, by human beings shall their blood be shed; for in the image of God has God made humankind" (Gen. 9:6). Murder always mars the image of God and is the antithesis of God's command to fill the earth with image-bearers (Gen. 9:7).

The next two chapters of Genesis contain two important pieces of the biblical picture this book is highlighting. At first glance, these chapters might not seem connected, but they are. The writer of Genesis was using a literary device where he showed the result of a situation before explaining the situation. It would be like seeing a friend you had not talked to in years and she exclaims, "I got married!" and then proceeds to tell the story of meeting the man of her dreams, how he proposed, how beautiful the wedding was, and now they are married. Genesis chapter ten is called the Table of Nations in some translations. It is the listing of the nations that were created as a result of Genesis chapter eleven, which is the more familiar story of the tower of Babel. There are seventy (or seventy-two some say) nations listed in chapter ten. This is an important fact for a later chapter. For now, simply note that the first important piece of the picture is that the nations were created as a result of Babel.

The second thing to note is the motivation of the people in chapter eleven. In verse four they said, "Come, let us build for ourselves a city with a tower that reaches to the heavens, so that we may make a name for ourselves and not be scattered over the face of the whole earth." One can hear the pride in their plan, the defiance, and the selfish ambition. However, it is more than just that. They were determined to make a name *for themselves*, as opposed to being image-bearers of God. They determined to *avoid* being scattered over the earth, as opposed to God's repeated command to "fill the earth" (Gen. 1:28; 9:1, 7). The tower of Babel stood in direct opposition to God's command, highlighting once again mankind's propensity to define good and evil on their own terms. Therefore, the Lord created a multitude of languages, thus undermining their ability to communicate. Then, He scattered the newly formed nations, listed in chapter ten, all over the earth (Gen. 11:9).

A mere eleven chapters into God's story, we see the beauty and intentionality of creation, God's desire for His image to fill the earth, and the importance of relationship between man and God, man and woman, and man and creation. However, we also see the propensity of mankind to disregard God's plan and insist upon his own way, wickedness and sin spiraling out of control, and mankind moving further and further away from God. But God. He would not leave them. He would not let them live without hope of restored relationship with Him. He would not let them live eternally in their shame and sin, nor would He let them die without hope. He would prove to be the God of reconciliation by always providing the path to redemption. And it would all begin with one man.

The Covenant

THE ABRAHAMIC COVENANT

Genesis chapter twelve has been called the turning point of God's story. One could even say that it is the turning point of all human history. Ralph Winters has been credited with calling the first eleven chapters the introduction to the Bible.[1] As we will see, this is where God initiates a plan that will be the undoing of everything that had gone wrong thus far in the story. Chapter eleven ended with genealogy from Shem, one of the righteous sons of Noah, to a man named Abram. Often when we come to long lists of genealogy in Scripture, we roll our eyes and skim through it quickly. They can certainly be mind-numbingly boring at times; however, genealogy records highlight the fact that these are not made-up stories and fairytales. These were real historical figures, actual people who lived and died. We might not know much about Serug, the great-grandfather of Abram (Gen. 11:22-23), but if his story had been relevant to understanding the story God has been writing since the beginning of time, we would. What we do know is that he lived and was a part of the ancestral line that led from Adam to Shem to Abram, a line that would eventually be shown as a small part of the connection between Adam, the son of God, and Jesus, the Son of God (Luke 3:23-37).

Scripture introduces us to Abram using only his ancestral line, the name of his

---

[1] Ralph Winter, "The 'First Chapter' of the Bible: Genesis 12–50," (WCF Lecture, around 1995, as World Christian Foundations curriculum was being developed).

barren wife (Sarai), and where they lived, which was called Harran (Gen. 11:27-32). Nothing is said of his character, his faith, or how he caught the eye of the God of the universe. He seems, from Scripture, to be a fairly unremarkable, normal guy. Yet, God would change the course of all human history through this one man.

Chapter twelve begins with the Lord telling Abram to leave his home, his family, and his people to venture off to an unknown land (Gen. 12:1). That simply did not happen. In fact, for most of human history and still today in many cultures, people do not just pack up and move to unknown lands away from their family. How would he live? Who would offer protection to him and his wife? Then for the first time, we catch a glimpse of Abram's character when in obedience he simply goes (Gen. 12:4). In between the calling and the going, something very important happened. God made a promise to Abram that revealed His purpose, unrolling His plan like a red carpet leading to this unknown land. God said:

> I will make you into a great nation,
> and I will bless you.
> I will make your name great,
> and you will be a blessing.
> I will bless those who bless you,
> and whoever curses you I will curse;
> and all peoples on earth
> will be blessed through you (Gen. 12:2-3).

This is the Abrahamic Covenant. John Mark Comer calls it "the fulcrum point for the entire Old Testament."[2] John Stott calls these the most unifying verses in the entire Bible because as he says it, the whole of God's purpose is encapsulated here.[3] Not only do I wholeheartedly agree with that statement, I would add to it that these are also some of the most misunderstood and misquoted verses in all of Scripture (thus the purpose of writing this book). This is one of the primary verses used by those who believe a curse will come from God to those who choose not to stand with modern-day Israel. There is much more Scripture to cover before we can even

---

[2] John Mark Comer, *God has a Name* (Grand Rapids, MI: Zondervan, 2017), 199.

[3] John R. W. Stott, "The Living God is a Missionary God," in *Perspectives on the World Christian Movement: A Reader* (Pasadena, CA: William Carey Library, 2009), 3.

begin to address that question, but we will get there. For now, let's start by breaking down some of the components.

First, God said that He would make Abram into a great nation. Interestingly, even with what little we know about Abram, Scripture has already highlighted two things that make this seem unlikely, if not impossible. God told Abram to leave his family and people. This is not the start of a great nation. Human wisdom would say that he needs to at least start as a large tribe to become a great nation. Instead, he was asked to be a lone ranger in a foreign land. Furthermore, his wife, Sarai, was childless and unable to conceive (Gen. 11:30). Whether Abram looked up or down his own generational line, nothing seemed to indicate that a great nation could come from him.

Next, God spoke blessing and favor over Abram. He promised to make his name great, to bless him, and that he would be seen as blessed by others. He also promised to bless those who act favorably toward Abram and curse anyone who did not. Those are tremendous promises! What favor Abram had stumbled upon! Whether it speaks to his faith or simple practicality, he was wise to agree to follow the Lord with promises of blessing like this.

Lastly, and most importantly, the promises came with purpose. God did not simply say that He would pour out lavish blessings on Abram and his descendants out of mere favoritism. God did not say, "Follow me and be blessed" with an exclamation point or even a period at the end of the sentence. He said, "Follow me and be blessed…so that all peoples on earth will be blessed *through you*" (Gen. 12:3, paraphrase mine). There was a purpose in the blessing. God was going to use Abram and his descendants to bless the whole world!

Personally, I would have had a lot of questions. What exactly do you mean by that Lord? How will You bless the whole world through me? How will I become a great nation? Why me?? What's the catch here? Surely there's something I need to do in order to earn this favor. However, Scripture does not record Abram asking anything. He simply "went, as the Lord had told him" (Gen. 12:4). What faith.

The land was called Canaan. It was filled with Canaanites, as one might imagine. The Canaanites were the wicked, cursed descendants of Noah's youngest son, Ham. When Ham shamed his father in front of Noah's other two sons, Noah cursed Ham's son Canaan (Gen. 9:20-25). Although the Canaanites were cursed, the land they possessed was a good land and strategically positioned for God's unfurling plan. Upon arrival to the land, God told Abram that the land would be given to his offspring (Gen. 12:7). Despite the barrenness of his wife, Abram trusted God and built Him an altar.

In chapter thirteen, Abram and his nephew Lot, who had accompanied him, parted ways. Abram offered Lot his choice of land and Lot, in a shameful and disrespectful act, chose the land that appeared better. Yet, after they parted ways, the Lord reassured Abram that His blessing and favor were still upon him. He told Abram to look all around him and said, "All the land that you see I will give to you and your offspring forever. I will make your offspring like the dust of the earth, so that if anyone could count the dust, then your offspring could be counted" (Gen. 13:15-16). Yet, Sarai remained childless.

Not until chapter fifteen did Abram start questioning God's promises and plan. He had obediently followed and listened to the promises spoken, even though he could not see how they would come to pass. Finally, he said, "Sovereign Lord, what can you give me since I remain childless and the one who will inherit my estate is Eliezer of Damascus? … You have given me no children; so a servant in my household will be my heir" (Gen. 15:2-3). Ironically, the name Eliezer in Hebrew is Eli'ezer, which literally means "my God is help" or "God of help."[4] He was, in effect, saying, "God how can You help when my servant named 'my God is help' appears to be the only solution here?" I wonder how often we do that to God. We doubt Him even when the answer is right before our eyes. In loving, Paternal gentleness, God reassured Abram that this man would not be his heir, but rather a natural-born son from his own body (Gen. 15:4). Then in the same manner that He had once told Abram that his descendants would outnumber the dust, He said that they would also outnumber the stars in sky (Gen. 15:5).

Big promises from a big God to a human man with only human eyes to see his circumstances. And yet, "Abram believed the Lord, and he credited it to him as righteousness" (Gen. 15:6). The rest of chapter fifteen is rich with prophecy and hope. Abram asked God how he could be sure that he would possess the land that the Lord promised (Gen. 15:8). A valid question for a man without a family. The

---

[4] "Eliezer," *Behind the Name*, June 9, 2023. https://www.behindthename.com/name/eliezer; "Eliezer meaning." *Abarim Publications*, November 22, 2023. https://www.abarim-publications.com/Meaning/Eliezer.html.

The Covenant

Lord responded by having Abram gather up a few specific animals, cut them in half, and arrange the pieces in two parallel lines (Gen. 15:9-10). The sun began to set and "Abram fell into a deep sleep, and a thick and dreadful darkness came over him" (Gen. 15:12). What Abram knew in that moment is not initially clear to the casual reader of Scripture. However, when we understand what God was doing, it is probably a safe assumption that Abram was maybe wrestling with a reasonable number of nerves over what he knew was about to happen.

In this time, there was a common cultural practice called cutting the covenant. When two people would enter into a covenant with one another, they engaged in this practice. They would come together and take a few animals that would be sacrificed and cut in half. The halves would then be arranged in parallel lines. The two people entering the covenant would then walk between the pieces together, weaving their casual stroll in between the carcasses of the slain animals. As they did that, no doubt with blood covering the pathways they walked, they would state their mutual understanding of the covenant that they were making. The dead animals were symbolic of the severity of breaking the covenant. It was also a visual reminder of what the covenantal partner could do to the one who broke the covenant. "I promise that I will do (insert promise) and if I do not keep up my end of the covenant, you get to do to me what we have done to these animals. And vice versa, if you do not keep your end, you are dead meat (pun intended)." Brutal and unusual as it may seem to us, this was a common practice in Abram's time. When God told him to gather the animals and cut them up, we can assume that Abram knew what was happening.

However, Abram did not walk through the pieces. He slept. While he slept, "a smoking firepot with a blazing torch appeared and passed between the pieces" (Gen. 15:17). Both the smoking firepot and the blazing torch represent the Lord. God walked through the pieces on His own. "On that day the Lord made a covenant with Abram" (Gen. 15:18), but Abram did not make the covenant with the Lord. By God figuratively representing Himself as both parties, He was essentially telling Abram that He was going to keep the covenant regardless of Abram's involvement or that of his descendants. The only blood at risk of being shed here was God's.[5]

God revealed to Abram that His plan to bless the whole world through Abram was

---
[5] Comer, *God Has a Name*, 199-203.

not contingent on Abram or his descendants. God was going to do it. Furthermore, it would involve giving all of the land from the Nile River to the Euphrates to Abram's descendants (Gen. 15:18). The significance of that will be revisited in a later chapter. The Lord also prophetically told Abram that "for four hundred years [his] descendants [would] be strangers in a country not their own and that they [would] be enslaved and mistreated there" (Gen. 15:13). Abram would be long gone by then, but God assured him that when the sin of those in possession of the land of promise, the Amorites, had "reached its full measure," God would deliver Abram's descendants out of slavery and into the promised land (Gen. 15:16). This promised land would become pivotal to God's plan of redeeming all of humanity.

THE SONS OF ABRAM

At this point in Scripture, the covenant is full of promise and hope. God had promised to bless Abram abundantly, using him as a conduit of blessing for the entire earth. He reassured Abram that he would in fact have children and that eventually they would possess the land that God had promised Abram. God had reiterated the promise and cut Himself into a covenantal obligation to fulfill it. Yet still, Abram and Sarai remained childless. Personally, having endured two separate seasons of infertility, I can only imagine the emotions Sarai must have been feeling. Her husband had all of these amazing blessings spoken over Him by God, and yet it seemed with human eyes that it was Sarai's fault that none of it could actually come to fruition.

Sarai's story of infertility is crucial for the story of Israel. In Genesis chapter sixteen, Sarai reached her breaking point of not being able to bring forth God's promises to Abram. We could easily judge her for thinking that God needed her help and intervention in order to keep His covenant with her husband, but truth be told, nearly every one of us have been or will be forced at some point to make decisions like this. Do we wait upon the Lord despite the ever-increasing improbability? Do we step out in faith and take action? There is certainly a fine line of discernment here. Sarai's actions were not necessarily immoral (because there was no defined law yet) and they were acceptable within the cultural context of that time (not that culture should dictate morality standards). But did she wait upon the Lord in faith, or did she take matters into her own hands?

Sarai said to Abram, "The Lord has kept me from having children. Go, sleep with my servant; perhaps I can build a family through her" (Gen. 16:2). Her plan worked and her Egyptian servant, Hagar, became pregnant. However, as one might expect, tensions began to rise between the two women after that (Gen. 16:4-6). Eventually, Sarai sent Hagar away. While she was fleeing, an angel of the Lord found her and ministered to her in her distress (Gen. 16:7-9). The angel told her to go back to Abram and Sarai and said to her, "I will increase your descendants so much that they will be too numerous to count" (Gen. 16:10). This is precisely what God had spoken over Abram, likening his descendants to the dust of the earth (Gen. 13:15-16) and the stars of the sky (Gen. 15:5). The angel also told her to name the son she carried Ishmael, which means "God hears" (Gen. 16:11).

What happened next is remarkably beautiful on multiple levels. Hagar gave a name to the Lord. She called Him "El Roi," which means "the God who sees me" (Gen. 16:13). She said, "I have now seen the One who sees me" (Gen. 16:13). Remarkably, this is the first time in the Scriptures that God is ascribed a name. Not only that, but it was given to Him by a woman. A female servant in the midst of perhaps the hardest time of her life. She was feeling neglected, mistreated, abused, forgotten, and outcast. Yet, the Lord met her and made her feel seen. Furthermore, this is the only place in Scripture where He is called El Roi. This was a special interaction for sure.

Lastly, and perhaps most importantly for this writing, Hagar's son Ishmael would be the lineage from Abram that would become the Arab people, and eventually the Muslim faith. It is important to understand this truth at this point in the story, even though it may seem a bit anachronistic since the Muslim faith would not be birthed for almost 3,000 years. One cannot say conclusively if it was within God's will for Abram to conceive a child with Hagar as it was initiated by the prompting of Sarai, not the Lord speaking it to Abram. Regardless, God chose to bless Ishmael as well. The next chapter will provide some clarity on that blessing.

Chapter seventeen is another important chapter in the covenant between Abram and the Lord. God reiterated to the ninety-nine-year-old Abram that He was establishing a covenant with him and would "greatly increase [his] numbers" (Gen. 17:2). God told Abram that he would be "the father of many nations" (Gen. 17:4) and then He changed his name from Abram to Abraham. Abram means "exalted father," but Abraham means "father of many." The distinction is subtle but important.

Although his name had always been "exalted father," he had only just become a father at the age of eighty-six. Then, thirteen years later, God called him "father of many." God also spoke His covenantal blessing over him again, this time over Abraham, not Abram:

> I have made you a father of many nations. I will make you very fruitful; I will make nations of you, and kings will come from you. I will establish my covenant as an everlasting covenant between me and you and your descendants after you for generations to come, to be your God and the God of your descendants after you. The whole land of Canaan, where you now reside as a foreigner, I will give as an everlasting possession to you and your descendants after you; and I will be their God (Gen. 17:5-8).

This was now the third time in Scripture that God had spoken this over Abram, who from this point on would be known as Abraham.

This time, however, there was a required sign of agreement on the part of Abraham, and it was no small ask. This was when God called Abraham to undergo circumcision as "the sign of the covenant" (Gen. 17:10-11). Imagine for a moment Abraham's thought process as he received this news. He had been following the Lord faithfully since He called him from his country and his people. He had all of these amazing promises, blessings, and covenant spoken over him. He was certainly not a father of many yet, having only conceived one son through a woman who was not his wife. Now in a late-game surprise move, God asked him to cut the very part of his body that is required to biologically become a father of any. Regardless of one's personal opinions on circumcision today, it is at least a culturally normative practice in most parts of the modern world. However, back then, this was unheard of.

I have two sons who were both circumcised shortly after birth. It was done in a hospital with anesthesia. Although they were both a little fussy after the procedure, the recovery seemed to cause them no pain or irritation. We were told by the doctor that the procedure on infants is not that painful, but it becomes more and more painful as boys get older. Because of this, performing it on a newborn is highly recommended. When God introduced circumcision to Abraham, He was asking a ninety-nine-year-old man and his thirteen-year-old son, Ishmael, to undergo this never-before-heard of, seemingly barbaric act of obedience. Furthermore, every male in the household was also required to participate, including servants (Gen. 17:23-27). Talk about harsh working conditions. Scripture seems to indicate that Abraham performed the procedure on himself and on all of the men and boys. I think I speak for most men in stating that this was probably Abraham's most heroic act of obedience up to that point.

In the midst of the name and anatomy change, God also said, "As for Sarai your wife, you are no longer to call her Sarai; her name will be Sarah. I will bless her and will surely give you a son by her. I will bless her so that she will be the mother of nations; kings of peoples will come from her" (Gen. 17:15-16). Scripture does not indicate the meaning of her name before or after the change and commentaries abound on interpretations, yet no universally accepted opinion can be found. I will refrain from offering an opinion on the subject other than to say that the season was changing for both Abram and Sarai. They were together stepping into the calling God had placed on their lives and He gave them both new identities in preparation for the season ahead.

The next part of the story is important to understand. As God was telling Abraham that he and Sarah would conceive a son, Abraham laughed at the thought of a man of one hundred years and a woman of ninety conceiving a child (Gen. 17:17). Then he said, "If only Ishmael might live under your blessing!" (Gen. 17:18). Abraham was essentially saying to the Lord, "I already have a son. Can we not just fulfill this plan through him and spare us from being centenarian parents of a newborn?" In response, God said:

> **Yes, but your wife Sarah will bear you a son, and you will call him Isaac. I will establish my covenant with him as an everlasting covenant for his descendants after him. And as for Ishmael, I have heard you: I will surely bless him; I will make him fruitful and will greatly increase his numbers. He will be the father of twelve rulers, and I will make him into a great nation. *But my covenant I will establish with Isaac*, whom Sarah will bear to you by this time next year (Gen. 17:19-21, emphasis added).**

God is very clear about what the role of each of Abraham's sons would be. They would *both* be blessed, fruitful, and the fathers of many. However, the covenant that had long since been established between God and Abraham would continue through the line of Isaac, not Ishmael. The means through which God would reconcile the world to Himself would come through Isaac. Although they would both be blessed, Isaac would be the son of the promise and of the covenant.

In the next chapter, God reiterated the promise. Three heavenly visitors appeared in the camp of Abraham and shared the news with Sarah about her forthcoming pregnancy (Gen. 18:10-15). The visit was a brief pitstop on their journey down to Sodom and Gomorrah, where they would bring forth God's judgment on the wicked. In whatever form God took to be there in the flesh, He said to His companions:

> Shall I hide from Abraham what I am about to do? Abraham will surely become a great and powerful nation, and all nations on earth will be blessed through him. For I have chosen him, so that he will direct his children and his household after him to keep the way of the Lord by doing what is right and just, so that the Lord will bring about for Abraham what he has promised him (Gen. 18:17-19).

The wording here mirrors that of the original covenant when God called Abram in Genesis chapter twelve. He would become a great nation and be blessed by God *so that* all the nations on earth would be blessed through him and his descendants. God was going to use the nation that would come from Abraham and his soon-to-be-conceived son, Isaac, to bless the entire earth.

Furthermore, the wording speaks a bit more to the essence of the blessing that God wanted to disseminate throughout the earth. Whenever the Scriptures say "so that," one can discern purpose in the statement. The statement following "so that" is the purpose of the statement preceding it. God chose Abraham *so that* he would teach his descendants the way of the Lord (Gen. 18:19). This was reconciliatory. Everything that mankind had done in opposition of God's initial plan for relationship with His creation was going to be undone through the descendants of Abraham. Reconciliation with the Lord was the essence of the blessing that the descendants of Abraham would initiate throughout the nations of the earth. God was going to use this man and his descendants to redeem the brokenness of mankind and restore the relationship between God and man back to the original intent.

THE PATRIARCHS

Up to this point, we have taken a fairly deep dive into each of the first eighteen chapters of Genesis. My intention here is not to write a commentary on the entire Bible, so you will see that the rest of the story will not look as deeply into Scripture verse-by-verse. The important themes that have been uncovered are the fall and decline of mankind, and God's redemption plan that had begun to unfold through the covenant He made with Abraham. Christianity, Judaism, and Islam all claim Abraham as the patriarch or father of their faith; however, those three major world religions eventually branch off into three distinctly different and opposing faiths. The Christian and Jewish branch track together all the way until the first century A.D. The Muslim branch runs in a somewhat parallel branch until the late 800s A.D. We will talk more about all three as we continue to study the thread of God's big story throughout the Scriptures.

Genesis chapter twenty-one finally brings about the long-anticipated birth of Isaac, whose name means "laughter." Sarah said, "God has brought me laughter, and everyone who hears about this will laugh with me" (Gen. 21:6). Laughter of joy for Sarah, who finally bore a child, and joyful but perhaps comedic laughter over the idea of a woman in her nineties actually conceiving a baby (Gen. 18:12; 21:6). After a few years, however, the laughter was disrupted by yet another round of relational tension between Sarah and Hagar. Hagar and Ishmael were still a part of the family and tribe of Abraham. At the feast thrown in honor of Isaac's weaning, Ishmael was caught by Sarah mocking her precious Isaac (Gen. 21:8-9). Sarah demanded that Abraham send Hagar and Ishmael away, declaring that Ishmael would never share Isaac's inheritance (Gen. 21:10).

Although Sarah had done this before when Hagar was pregnant, her actions this time greatly distressed Abraham (Gen. 21:11). Ishmael would have been around twenty years old at this point and Abraham loved him. God reassured Abraham to do what Sarah had asked and to not worry. He said, "It is through Isaac that your offspring will be reckoned. I will make the son of [Hagar] into a nation also, because he is your offspring" (Gen. 21:12-13). As Hagar and Ishmael wandered the desert, they ran out of water and Hagar feared death for herself and her son. Once again, the Lord met her in her distress.

Scripture says that Hagar wept, but it does not record her praying or calling out to God. Yet, He heard the cries of Ishmael and sent an angel to Hagar (Gen. 21:17). The angel said, "Do not be afraid; God has heard the boy crying as he lies there. Lift the boy up and take him by the hand, for I will make him into a great nation" (Gen. 21:17-18). Ishmael was not the child of the promise or of the covenant, but that did not mean that he was despised or rejected by God. This was the second time God had shown up for Hagar. God declared to Abraham more than once that His intentions were good for Ishmael and his descendants. Furthermore, Scripture is clear that "God was with [Ishmael] as he grew up" (Gen. 21:20). Sarah may have rejected Ishmael, but God had not.

Much has been written, spoken, and taught about Genesis chapter twenty-two in which God asked Abraham to do the unthinkable: sacrifice the child of promise, Isaac. This test required more faith than leaving his country and his family, more faith than the covenant of circumcision, and more faith than decades of waiting on a promise that appeared impossible. If God actually allowed Isaac to die, the slate would have been wiped clean. Would Sarah have been able to conceive again now that she was a centenarian herself? Theologians for centuries have theorized on Abraham's understanding of the situation. Perhaps he knew God would provide a substitutionary sacrifice, like he told Isaac (Gen. 22:8). Perhaps he thought if he did sacrifice Isaac, God would raise him from the dead. Verse five certainly seems to indicate that he believed both he and Isaac would come back. But perhaps he was lying when he said, "We will worship and *we* will come back to you" (Gen. 22:5, emphasis added). Regardless of what he believed in his head and heart to be true, he put his long-awaited son of promise on the altar and "took the knife to slay his son" (Gen. 22:9-10). Would I have gotten that close? Could I trust God with my most cherished earthly blessing? Abraham's calling and destiny required this recklessly abandoned faith in God and God alone. What could God do through you or through me with that level of faith?

Thankfully Abraham passed the test and God did not make him actually slay his beloved son. Then God said to him:

> I swear by myself, declares the Lord, that because you have done this and have not withheld your son, your only son, I will surely bless you and make your descendants as numerous as the stars in the sky and as the sand on the seashore. Your descendants

will take possession of the cities of their enemies, and through your offspring all nations on earth will be blessed, because you have obeyed me (Gen. 22:16-18).

This was now the seventh time that God had confirmed His promise to Abraham. The promise of blessing, that included the promised land, for the purpose of blessing all nations on earth. The importance of this covenant in God's eyes cannot be overstated. Although He had repeated it multiple times, made it clear that He would keep the covenant regardless of the involvement of Abraham or his descendants, and marked Abraham and his descendants with a physical sign of the covenant (circumcision), this was the first time that God swore by Himself. He was putting His own name on the line.

God's name was and is very important to Him. He would later declare "the holiness of [His] great name" through the prophet Ezekiel (Ez. 36:23). He would tell His people through the prophet Isaiah, "How can I let myself be defamed? I will not yield my glory to another" (Is. 48:11). He would decree to His people, "Do not profane my holy name, for I must be acknowledged as holy" (Lev. 22:32) and "They must be holy to their God and must not profane the name of their God" (Lev. 21:6). Yet, here He put His holy name on the line. For the sake of His holy name, He would keep the covenant, no matter the cost. All nations of the earth would be blessed.

After the death of Sarah in Genesis twenty-three, Abraham sent his servant to find a wife for Isaac among his own people (Gen. 24:2-4). He stood firm on the promises made to him by God and the promises he himself had made to God in the selection criteria for Isaac's wife. First, she must be from among Abraham's people, not from among the Canaanite women who were not followers of Yahweh. Second, Isaac would not return to Abraham's home country because the land of Canaan was promised to him (Gen. 24:6-8). The servant was successful in his assignment and found a woman named Rebekah to marry Isaac (Gen. 24:10-59). Before she left her family to go to an unknown land to marry an unknown man, her family spoke this blessing over her: "Our sister, may you increase to thousands upon thousands; may your offspring possess the cities of their enemies" (Gen. 24:60). What a prophetic declaration over the woman who would marry into the covenant of Abraham!

Before Abraham's death, he remarried and had more sons, but he "left everything he owned to Isaac" (Gen. 25:5). Isaac and Ishmael came together and buried Abraham with his beloved wife Sarah (Gen. 25:7-10). Scripture then shows the account of Ishmael's family line. He also had twelve sons, which fulfilled what God had spoken to Abraham in Genesis 17:20 (Gen. 25:12-18). The book of Genesis continues with the story of the patriarchs, Abraham, Isaac, and Jacob. They are called the patriarchs because they would become the fathers of the Jewish and Christian faith.

Isaac came next in the story and ironically, he also married a woman who was childless for an unknown amount of time. After he prayed for his wife, the Lord opened her womb, and she was able to conceive (Gen. 25:20-21). Rebekah gave birth to twins, Esau and Jacob. Esau was the first to emerge at birth and therefore the oldest. This is important to note because in a patriarchal society, the firstborn male was given a greater portion of his father's inheritance, as well as a greater amount of familial responsibility. However, in this case, the Lord had told Rebekah that "the older will serve the younger" (Gen. 25:23). Esau ended up giving up his birthright to his brother Jacob in a moment of desperate carnality. In that society, a person's birthright was one of their most valuable possessions, and yet a famished Esau gave his up to his brother in exchange for a single bowl of stew (Gen. 25:27-34).

Although Isaac had been called the child of the covenant since before he was conceived, Scripture does not show God speaking the covenant to him or over him until chapter twenty-six. Isaac had planned to leave the land of promise because of a famine, but the Lord appeared to him and told him not to (Gen. 26:1-3). The Lord then said:

> **Stay in this land for a while, and I will be with you and will bless you. For to you and your descendants I will give all these lands and will confirm the oath I swore to your father Abraham. I will make your descendants as numerous as the stars in the sky and will give them all these lands, and through your offspring *all nations on earth will be blessed*, because Abraham obeyed me and did everything I required of him, keeping my commands, my decrees and my instructions (Gen. 26:3-5, emphasis added).**

This is the same promise for the same purpose: God would bless Isaac with land and countless descendants in order to bless the entire world. Later in the chapter, God reiterated the promise when Isaac faced a fearful situation. He said, "Do not be afraid, for I am with you; I will bless you and will increase the number of your descendants for the sake of my servant Abraham" (Gen. 26:24). The thread of the blessing continued.

Even though Jacob had tricked Esau into giving up his birthright, Isaac still had every intention of speaking blessing over Esau as the firstborn. This was customary and very powerful. You have perhaps heard the phrase "a man's word is his bond." This was genuinely true back then. However, on Isaac's deathbed when he went to speak blessing over Esau, Rebekah and Jacob hatched up a scheme for Jacob to receive the firstborn blessing. Deceptively dressed as Esau, Jacob went into Isaac's room and convinced his father that he was, in fact, Esau (Gen. 27:1-27). With failing eyesight, Isaac was convinced, and he spoke over him, "May nations serve you and peoples bow down to you. Be lord over your brothers, and may the sons of your mother bow down to you. May those who curse you be cursed and those who bless you be blessed" (Gen. 27:29). The last line of that blessing is straight from the Abrahamic covenant, the same words God had spoken over Jacob's grandfather when He called him from his country and his people in chapter twelve, verses two and three. And although Jacob intended to speak it over Esau, his word was his bond, and it could not be revoked. Jacob, whose name means deceiver, proved to be quite exceptional at it.

Rebekah insisted upon finding a wife for Jacob among her own people instead of the cursed (and immoral) Canaanite women (Gen. 28:1-2). Before he left, Isaac blessed him again, this time knowing that he was blessing Jacob and not Esau. He said, "May God Almighty bless you and make you fruitful and increase your numbers until you become a community of peoples. May he give you and your descendants the blessing given to Abraham, so that you may take possession of the land where you now reside as a foreigner, the land God gave to Abraham (Gen. 28:3-4). In a similar manner to how God told Abraham that his second-born son would be the child of the covenant, Isaac's second-born also became the recipient and carrier of the covenant.

God Himself confirmed that the covenant would continue through Jacob. On his way to find a wife (or wives, as it would turn out), Jacob encountered God at a place he would call Bethel, meaning "house of God" (Gen. 28:10-15). The Lord spoke to him in a dream and said:

> **I am the Lord, the God of your father Abraham and the God of**

Isaac. I will give you and your descendants the land on which you are lying. Your descendants will be like the dust of the earth, and you will spread out to the west and to the east, to the north and to the south. *All peoples on earth will be blessed through you and your offspring* (Gen. 28:13-14, emphasis added).

Again, the wording highlights the same promise and the same purpose. Jacob and his descendants would be blessed in order to bless the entire world.

Scripture shares a lot of Jacob's life story. With twists and turns in the plot, heroism and deceit, scandal and love, it reads like a great movie. As with all of Scripture, I encourage you to dive in yourself and read God's story. This writing is meant to merely be a tool in helping you understand the overarching story, the grand narrative that informs the purpose of all the stories within. As for Jacob's life story, I will highlight only the parts important to the covenant and skim over the others.

Jacob ended up marrying two sisters, one of which he loved very much and the other he was tricked into marrying (Gen. 29). Karma is not a Christian tenet, but reaping what one sows certainly is. It appears that Jacob the deceiver finally got a dose of what he had sowed in his younger years. From his two wives, Rachel and Leah, plus their two servants, Zilpah and Bilhah, Jacob ended up fathering twelve sons (Gen. 29—30). After some time, the Lord called Jacob to leave the land of his wives' father and return to the land of his own family (Gen. 31:3). Along the way, Jacob had a unique encounter with God.

He was preparing to meet Esau for the first time since he had left to find a wife. Years had passed, but he was afraid that Esau would still be mad about the deceptive gain of his birthright and blessing. The night before they would meet, Jacob ended up encountering God in a bit of a wrestling match (Gen. 32:22-30). Jacob said he would not leave without a blessing and in turn, God said, "Your name will no longer be Jacob, but Israel, because you have struggled with God and with human beings and have overcome" (Gen. 32:26, 28). Victor P. Hamilton notes that "Jacob obtained Isaac's blessing through duplicity, but he can obtain God's blessing only by honest and prayerful request."[6] Just as God had done in changing Abram to Abraham,

---

[6] Victor P. Hamilton, *Handbook on the Pentateuch: Genesis, Exodus, Leviticus, Numbers, Deuteronomy* (Grand Rapids, MI: Baker Academic, 2015), 116.

God changed Jacob to Israel. Jacob was stepping into a new season and was, therefore, given a new identity. Hamilton also notes that with the new name came new character. "The name "Jacob" is as much *what* he is as *who* he is."[7] Now he would no longer be Jacob the deceiver but rather, Israel, he who struggled or strived to receive God's blessing.

Genesis thirty-five again notes the new name given to Jacob. Then the Lord said, "I am God Almighty; be fruitful and increase in number. A nation and a community of nations will come from you, and kings will come from your body. The land I gave to Abraham and Isaac I also give to you, and I will give this land to your descendants after you" (Gen. 35:11-12). In this promise and blessing we see first the original command given to Adam and then to Noah: be fruitful and multiply. Fill the earth with image-bearers of the One True God. Second, there is the promise of a nation that will come from the man now named Israel. God had told Rebekah that there were two nations in her womb when she carried Jacob and Esau (Gen. 25:23). Also, Isaac had said to Jacob, knowing he was speaking to Jacob, that he would become a community of people (Gen. 28:3). Lastly, we see the emphasis again on the land of promise. A nation was clearly coming with the promise of a land of their own for the purpose of blessing the entire world.

THE SONS OF ISRAEL

The stories of the twelve sons of Israel are some of the more frequently taught about, read about, and shared stories from the Old Testament. Veggie Tales and Superbook have made the stories come alive even to children in entertaining and captivating ways. I love a good story as much as the next person and these stories do not disappoint. For the purpose of this writing though, I want to hone in on only one of the twelve brothers: Joseph. Although Joseph was Israel's eleventh son, he was his father's favorite because he was the firstborn of his favorite wife, Rachel. Israel lavished gifts upon Joseph that the other sons did not receive, like the well-known richly ornamented robe or coat of many colors (Gen. 37:3). As brothers are prone to do, his older brothers became quite jealous of Joseph. That jealousy became full-on rage when Joseph had two dreams that seemed to indicate that they, along with their father Israel, would one day bow before Joseph (Gen. 37:4-11).

---

[7] Hamilton, *Handbook on the Pentateuch*, 116.

Everyone has their breaking point and that was it for the sons of Israel. They hatched up a plan to kill Joseph and cover up their crime. The oldest brother, Reuben, despite having a very questionable character (see Gen. 35:22), tried to rescue Joseph and bring him back to their father (Gen. 37:21-22). Then Judah came up with an even better plan. Why kill him when they could make a profit off of his life by selling him into slavery? I guess a brother really is born for adversity. So, Joseph was sold to a caravan of Ishmaelites headed for Egypt (Gen. 37:21-28). This part of the story and how Joseph fared in Egypt are well-known stories; however, the point that is often missed is how this all ties in with the Abrahamic Covenant.

God called Abraham to Canaan in His initial call in Genesis 12:1-3. God had told Isaac to stay in Canaan and *not* go to Egypt when there was a famine in their land (Gen. 26:2-3). God had also called Jacob back to Canaan from the land where he met his wives (Gen. 31:3). It would appear that God wanted the patriarchs in Canaan. However, through the story of Joseph, God called Israel and his entire family *out* of Canaan and *into* Egypt. Despite having gone into Egypt as a slave, Joseph rose to the rank of Pharoah's secondhand man (Gen. 41:41-43). Pharoah had two dreams for which God had given Joseph the interpretations, and this eventually led to Joseph singlehandedly preparing all of Egypt for an impending famine (Gen. 41:46-49). Then, when Israel and the rest of his family decided to go down to Egypt with Joseph, the Lord spoke to Israel saying, "I am God, the God of your father. Do not be afraid to go down to Egypt, for I will make you into a great nation there. I will go down to Egypt with you, and I will surely bring you back again" (Gen. 46:3-4). Of course, He would. God had already told Abraham that this would happen. When God was cutting the covenant with Abraham in Genesis chapter fifteen, God said, "Know for certain that for four hundred years your descendants will be strangers in a country not their own and that they will be enslaved and mistreated there. But I will punish the nation they serve as slaves, and afterward they will come out with great possessions ... In the fourth generation your descendants will come back here" (Gen. 15:13-16). God used Joseph to bring the sons of Israel to Egypt in order to fulfill what had been spoken to Abraham hundreds of years prior.

The Chosen People

THE EXODUS

Time went on and after relocating to Egypt, the sons of Israel went on to have sons and daughters of their own, as did those sons until this "exceeding fruitful" community of peoples became their very own nation, known as the nation of Israel, or the Israelites (Ex. 1:6-7). They began outnumbering their Egyptian hosts, and new kings with no connection to this nation replaced old kings who had shown them favor and kindness. One king said, "Look, the Israelites have become far too numerous for us. Come, we must deal shrewdly with them or they will become even more numerous and, if war breaks out, they will join our enemies, fight against us and leave the country" (Ex. 1:9-10). Thus, the nation of Israel became enslaved by the Egyptians.

At one point, the king decided to take drastic measures by enacting an infanticide among the male Hebrew babies (Ex. 1:15-22). However, we know of one well-known survivor: Moses. How ironic that that little baby boy, floating in a basket among the reeds, would drift right into the hands of the daughter of that murderous king? Moses, who was a Hebrew who had been raised as an Egyptian in Pharoah's palace, became uniquely positioned as Israel's deliverer.

Scripture does not say whether Moses was a follower of the God of the Hebrews or the gods of the Egyptians as he grew up in the palace, but his Hebrew roots and Egyptian upbringing did end up bringing trouble his way. After witnessing an Egyptian treating a Hebrew slave harshly, Moses killed the Egyptian and fled to a place called Midian (Ex. 2:11-15). He eventually got married there, had a family, and settled into a life far away from his past. One day, the God of the universe showed up in the form of a bush aflame and called the murderer in exile to a life of great purpose. He said, "I am the God of your father, the God of Abraham, the God of Isaac and the God of Jacob... I have indeed seen the misery of my people in Egypt...So I have come down to rescue them from the hand of the Egyptians and to bring them up out of that land into a good and spacious land, a land flowing with milk and honey" (Ex. 3:6, 8). This must have been a truly unbelievable moment for Moses. Then, because God seems to delight in using ordinary people to accomplish extraordinary things, He said, "So now, go. I am sending you to Pharoah to bring my people the Israelites out of Egypt" (Ex. 3:10).

Moses' reaction is exactly what one might expect from a guy who had spent a few decades hiding in the wilderness from the conflicting circumstances of his past. He said, "Who am I that I should go to Pharoah and bring the Israelites out of Egypt?" (Ex. 3:11) Perhaps you have asked God a similar question in a moment where God opened your eyes to the God-sized vision He has for your life. I know I have. Moses felt completely unqualified for the task.

Perhaps Abraham had felt the same way. God said, "I will be with you" (Ex. 3:12). That is really all any of us ever need to walk in what God calls us to. If His presence is with us, that is all the qualification we need. We have the benefit of knowing how the story unfolds. Moses boldly appeared before Pharoah, which ignited a series of miraculous plagues. He delivered God's people across a parted Red Sea, and then he led them through trials and tribulations in the wilderness. He became an exemplar of faith, intercession, and leadership. Yet, here we see him in his full humanity, afraid of the assignment and hesitant in his faith. "Who am I?" he asked. "What if they do not believe me or listen to me?" he questioned (Ex. 4:1). "But I have never been eloquent ... I am slow of speech and tongue," he wavered (Ex. 4:10). Even after God countered all of his hesitations, Moses still said, "Pardon your servant, Lord. Please send someone else" (Ex. 4:13). Moses only saw who he thought he was, not who God said he would become and most importantly, who God already was.

For the sake of the topic at hand, there are three things that need attention from the exodus story. First, when Moses appeared before Pharoah the first time, the Lord told him to say, "Israel is my firstborn son…let my son go, so he may worship me" (Ex. 4:22-23). This is the first time in Scripture that the nation of Israel is referred to as the Lord's son. There is a prevalent theme of firstborn sonship throughout Scripture. It is important to see that God is intervening in the history of this people in a powerful way. In chapter six, He said:

> I am the Lord. I appeared to Abraham, to Isaac and to Jacob as God Almighty, but by my name the Lord I did not make myself fully known to them. I also established my covenant with them to give them the land of Canaan, where they resided as foreigners. I will take you as my own people, and I will be your God. Then you will know that I am the Lord your God, who brought you out from under the yoke of the Egyptians. And I will bring you to the land I swore with uplifted hand to give to Abraham, to Isaac and to Jacob. I will give it to you as a possession. I am the Lord (Ex. 6:2-4, 7-8).

God was actively choosing the nation of Israel for Himself through the exodus.

Second, through the series of plagues that came, every one of them was a direct affront on the Egyptians' gods. This was a display of God's power meant to show that He is Yahweh, the One True God. He said, "I will bring judgment on all the gods of Egypt. I am the Lord" (Ex. 12:12). The Egyptians had a god of the Nile, so Yahweh turned the Nile River to blood (Ex. 7:14-24). They had a god personified as a frog, so Yahweh sent teems of frogs throughout the land (Ex. 8:1-15). They had a god of the earth, then from "the dust of the ground" came gnats (Ex. 8:16-19). They had a god of the sky, so from the sky came devastating thunder and hail (Ex. 9:13-35). In the midst of that particular plague, God said:

> Let my people go, so that they may worship me, or this time I will send the full force of my plagues against you and against your officials and your people, so you may know that there is no one like me in all the earth. For by now I could have stretched out my hand and struck you and your people with a plague that would have wiped you off the earth. But I have raised you up for

this very purpose, that I might show you my power and that my name might be proclaimed in all the earth (Ex. 9:13-16).

He certainly could have wiped out the Egyptians and delivered Israel much quicker and more efficiently. He did not, however, only want their deliverance. He wanted a mighty display of power that the nations would see or hear about. He wanted His name proclaimed in all the earth, and He desired to have people who bore His image and reflected His glory in all the earth. Remember, this has been God's ultimate purpose since the beginning. When He told Adam in Genesis 1:28 to be fruitful, multiply, and fill the earth with those who bore His image, He declared the purpose of creation. This purpose has never changed. He wants the whole world to know that He is God and He will not share His glory with any idol or false god.

Lastly, it is important to notice the reason why He told Pharoah to let His people go. When He first called Israel His firstborn son, He told Pharoah to let His son go "so he may worship me" (Ex. 4:23). His purpose is to gather worshipers. This phrase is repeated throughout the plagues:

- "Let my people go, so that they may worship me in the wilderness" (7:16)
- "Let my people go, so that they may worship me" (8:1)
- "So that you may know there is no one like the Lord our God" (8:10)
- "Let my people go, so that they may worship me" (8:20)
- "So that you will know that I, the Lord, am in this land" (8:22)
- "Let my people go, so that they may worship me" (9:1)
- "Let my people go, so that they may worship me" (9:13)
- "So that you may know that there is no one like me in all the earth" (9:14)
- "So you may know that the earth is the Lord's" (9:29)
- "And that you may know that I am the Lord" (10:2)
- "Let my people go, so that they may worship me" (10:3)
- "So that my wonders may be multiplied in Egypt" (11:9)

The Chosen People 34

He wants to be known and worshiped by *all* of His creation. The display of power was meant to bring Israel to Him as worshipers.

It was also meant to display His worthiness before the Egyptians and to gather worshipers from even among them. He said, "I will gain glory for myself through Pharoah and all his army, and the Egyptians will know that I am the Lord" (Ex. 14:4). Again, "I will gain glory through Pharoah and all his army…the Egyptians will know that I am the Lord" (Ex. 14:17-18). And it worked. When the Israelites left Egypt, "many other people went up with them" (Ex. 12:38). God gained reconciliation and gathered worshipers from among the Egyptians. Furthermore, "when the Israelites saw the great power the Lord displayed against the Egyptians, the people feared the Lord and put their trust in him" (Ex. 14:31). His purpose in the exodus was to gain glory from the nations and reconcile people to Himself.

The exodus did not only bring about worship from Israel and Egypt. It brought in worshipers from Midian, where Moses had lived after fleeing Egypt. Moses had sent his wife and sons back to Midian while he completed his mission in Egypt. After the exodus, his father-in-law, Jethro, met up with them on the other side of the Red Sea, bringing his family back to him. Jethro was a priest of Midian, a leader of pagan worship. However, he "heard of everything God had done for Moses and for his people Israel, and how the Lord had brought Israel out of Egypt" (Ex. 18:1). He was "delighted to hear about all the good things the Lord had done for Israel in rescuing them" (Ex. 18:9). In fact, because of the mighty display of Yahweh's power, Jethro ended up leaving behind his pagan beliefs and praising the God of the Hebrews! (Ex. 18:10) He said, "Now I know that the Lord is greater than all other gods, for he did this to those who had treated Israel arrogantly. Then Jethro, Moses' father-in-law, brought a burnt offering and other sacrifices to God" (Ex. 18:11-12). Israelites, Egyptians, and now Midianites were coming back to a reconciled relationship of worshiping Yahweh.

There's another story that highlights how the mighty acts of God in Egypt brought about worshipers from the nations. Moving forward in the Scriptures briefly to about forty years ahead, just before the Israelites were about to enter the land of promise, is the story of Rahab. Rahab was either a prostitute or an innkeeper in the city of Jericho (what an unfortunate confusion of vocation lost in translation to antiquity). When Moses' successor took some spies in to survey the land before entering through Jericho, Rahab became an unlikely ally for them, hiding them from her own people. She said:

> I know that the Lord has given you this land and that a great fear of you has fallen on us, so that all who live in this country are melting in fear because of you. We have heard how the Lord dried up the water of the Red Sea for you when you came out of Egypt ... When we heard of it, our hearts melted in fear and everyone's courage failed because of you, for the Lord your God is God in heaven above and on the earth below (Josh. 2:9-11).

The drying or parting of the Red Sea had occurred forty years ago in a land far enough away that it would have been almost a two-week direct journey from there to Jericho. Rahab might not have even been alive when that event happened. Yet here she was, proclaiming the praise of Yahweh because of the mighty display of His power. After the fall of Jericho, Rahab and her family were spared, and they joined the nation of Israel. Rahab, the Gentile, not only married into the Israelite nation, but became one of only five women included in Matthew's genealogy of Jesus!

Think back to the Abrahamic Covenant. God told Abraham that He would make him into a great nation and through this nation, all peoples of the earth would be blessed. From the very beginning of God choosing Israel as His own people, He began the work of blessing all nations with a right-standing relationship with Him *through* Israel. God had told Jacob/Israel, "All peoples on earth will be blessed through you and your offspring" (Gen. 28:14). And so, it had begun.

CHOSEN

At this point in the story, we have the descendants of Abraham, Isaac, and Jacob that had become too vast to count, united as the nation of Israel, and chosen by God as His firstborn son (Ex. 4:22-23). All of the promises of God to the patriarchs were finally coming into view. Throughout history, the Jewish people have self-identified and been known by others as "the chosen people." But why? Why did God choose them? Was there a purpose or a reason for the choosing, or was it simply favoritism? This is the key to understand how the Israelites would be a blessing to all nations of the earth.

After the exodus and miraculous deliverance from Egypt, Moses began leading the people into the desert and toward the land of promise. After about three months, they arrived at Mount Sinai. Moses went up the mountain and received a message from the Lord for His people. He said:

> You yourselves have seen what I did to Egypt, and how I carried you on eagles' wings and brought you to myself. Now if you obey me fully and keep my covenant, then out of all the nations you will be my treasured possession. Although the whole earth is mine, you will be for me a kingdom of priests and a holy nation (Ex. 19:4-6).

In a way, this moment was the choosing of the chosen people. God had established the covenant with Abraham, then with Isaac, then with Jacob/Israel. Now it was time to officially enter into the covenant with their descendants.

Hamilton breaks down the exchange by stating, "We pass from cause to effects, from divine love to human responsibility, and then from effects to results."[8] God intervened in their history and set them free from slavery. He brought them to Himself out of His love for them and His love for the patriarchs. It is important to note that the command to obey is not what brought salvation to Israel or a relationship between God and His people. At this point, God had not given the law yet. They had survived the plagues and crossed over the Red Sea. They had freedom and salvation from Egypt. God had already called Israel His firstborn son. Miriam, the sister of Moses, and the Israelites sang on the freedom shore of the Red Sea, "In your unfailing love you will lead the people you have redeemed" (Ex. 15:13). Love, salvation, and relationship all preceded the law.

The Israelites are the chosen nation of God, but this was where He told them why. There would be privilege in their relationship, they would be God's "treasured possession." There would also be responsibility in their relationship. They would be "a kingdom of priests and a holy nation." Think about the implications of this calling. What is the role of a priest? It is to bring people to God. It is to shepherd people into a better understanding of God that leads to a relationship with Him. God was calling the entire nation of Israel His priests to the rest of the world. Furthermore,

---

[8] Hamilton, *Handbook on the Pentateuch*, 185.

they would be holy, sanctified, and set apart. The law that was to come was meant to purify Israel, not save Israel, and through their purified "set apartness," their lives would glorify God before all the nations on the earth. Hamilton says, "Thus God's people are unique, separated from the world, but only that they may serve as ministers of reconciliation in that world."[9] If you take nothing else away from this book, let it be this: The nation of Israel was chosen to be ministers of reconciliation to the nations of the world in fulfillment of the Abrahamic Covenant. This was the purpose in their being chosen.

THE PROMISED LAND

There is a lot that happened between Mount Sinai and the promised land, some of which we will circle back to. However, in grasping this concept of why Israel was chosen and how it was meant to fulfill the Abrahamic Covenant, we must include a discussion on the promised land. The land of Canaan was where God called Abraham to reside after departing from his family and his father's country (Gen. 12:1). Abraham, Isaac, and Jacob all lived there as foreigners. God described it as all the land between the Nile and the Euphrates rivers (Gen. 15:18), which is not modern-day Israel, but more like all of the modern-day Arabian Peninsula. Thus far, He had described it as "a good and spacious land, a land flowing with milk and honey" (Ex. 3:8). What had not yet been apparent is why He chose this land for this people.

Throughout the course of history, every major trade route went through that plot of land. The Arabian Peninsula is the crossroads of Africa, Europe, and Asia. Any goods traveling between those continents would likely go through the promised land, whether by land or sea. The Great Silk Road is one of the most famous trade routes. Dmitry Voyakin describes the Great Silk Road this way:

> **The Great Silk Road is a system of caravan routes of ancient times and in the Middle Ages which connected Asia with the Mediterranean and European world. These routes highly influenced the development of trade interactions and cultural ties between the West and the East. The Silk Road served not only as route for exporting goods such as silk, spices, precious metals,**

---
[9] Hamilton, *Handbook on the Pentateuch*, 185.

minerals handicrafts, architecture and paintings but also transmitted cultural exchange including theatric performance, dance and music art. The Great Silk Road played moreover *a major role in dissemination of religions.* The Silk Road can thus be considered as an important fundament of human civilization. (Emphasis added)[10]

This major land trade route in history went right through the promised land. Furthermore, as a peninsula, sea trade routes surrounded the land. The Phoenicians, the Vikings, the Persians, the Greeks, the Romans, and every other major empire throughout history would have traveled by land and/or by sea throughout the promised land. This is precisely why God chose it.

Ezekiel 5:5, says, "This is Jerusalem, which I have set in the center of the nations." God was setting apart a people, uniquely and abundantly blessed, and placing them on center stage in the middle of the known world. Jesus would say it this way:

> You are the light of the world. A city on a hill cannot be hidden. Neither do people light a lamp and put it under a bowl. Instead they put it on a stand, and it gives light to everyone in the house. In the same way, let your light shine before others, that they may see your good deeds and glorify your Father in heaven (Matt. 5:14-16).

Through Israel, God was creating a city on a hill, a nation of priests set apart as holy, "a light for the Gentiles" (Is. 42:6), in the center of the known world. God's goodness on display for all the world to see. Before entering the land, Moses said:

> See, I have taught you decrees and laws as the Lord my God commanded me, so that you may follow them in the land you are entering to take possession of it. Observe them carefully, for this will show your wisdom and understanding *to the nations,* who will hear about all these decrees and say, "Surely this great nation is a wise and understanding people." What other nation is so great as to have their gods near them the way the Lord

---

[10] Dmitry Voyakin, "The Great Silk Road," *UNESCO.org,* 2024, https://en.unesco.org/silkroad/knowledge-bank/great-silk-road#:~:text=The%20Great%20Silk%20Road%20is,the%20West%20and%20the%20East.

our God is near us whenever we pray to him? (Deut. 4:5-7, emphasis added)

The exodus, the choosing of the chosen people, the promised land, and the law were all meant to bring the nations of the world back into relationship with Yahweh. These blessings were to be used to bless all nations of the earth (Gen. 12:3). To fulfill what had been promised to Abraham, Isaac, and Jacob. To undo the spiral of sin and shame that broke the relationship between God and His creation (Gen. 3).

THE LAW

Let us now return to post-exodus Mount Sinai where God had just set apart His "kingdom of priests and holy nation" (Ex. 19:6). God gave the people a choice in entering into the covenant with Him. It was not forced upon them. Moses went up the mountain to meet with God and basically received the conditions of the covenant. After he received that word from God, he "summoned the elders of the people and set before them all the words the Lord had commanded him to speak. The people all responded together, 'We will do everything the Lord has said.' So Moses brought their answer back to the Lord" (Ex. 19:7-8). This was like a marriage proposal to His beloved. He had proven His love through the exodus, He brought Israel to a holy mountain, took a knee down from heaven to earth, and asked if she wanted to be His. She said yes.

Then in an act not unlike a marriage ceremony, God told Israel to consecrate herself, saying her Bridegroom would be coming on the third day (Ex. 19:10-15). He descended the holy mountain and presented Himself to His people. The Israelites had washed clean from the journey and were wearing their best clothes. There was a majestic display of thunder and lightning as He came down amidst the trumpet blast (Ex. 19:16). There was smoke and fire, creating a reverent and holy atmosphere. The imagery is almost too beautiful to bear. Then, He spoke His vows to His bride: the Ten Commandments. Did that just ruin the imagery of the beautiful marriage ceremony, thinking of a list of laws as wedding vows? Do not let it. Try to let go of whatever rigid, legalistic, religious upbringing may have blemished your view of God's law so that we can look at it with fresh eyes.

The very first commandment is not unlike the vows most husbands and wives make on their wedding day. God asked His beloved to be faithful. Israel was to have no other gods before Him (Ex. 20:3). Commandments two and three are similar to the first: make no idols and honor the name of the Lord (Ex. 20:4-7). In the midst of these, He promised to show His love to "a thousand generations of those who love [Him] and keep [His] commandments" (Ex. 20:6). The fourth commandment is a gift, the gift of Sabbath rest. It is a promise of blessed and holy provision for those who trust in Him and cease striving (Ex. 20:8-11). Those first four had to do with being in holy relationship with a Holy God. The last six have to do with being in holy relationship with each other, as a community of faith.

The first four can be summarized by saying, "Love the Lord your God with all your heart and with all your soul and with all your mind," while the rest fall under "Love your neighbor as yourself" (Deut. 6:5; Lev. 19:18; Matt. 22:36-40). The fifth commandment came with a promise. Honor your parents *so that* "you may live long in the land the Lord your God is giving you" (Ex. 20:12). The sixth through tenth taught them how to love their neighbor. Do not kill, commit adultery, steal, lie, or covet. These are not meant to be exhaustive or touch on every potential problem a community faces. Rather, they are meant to be guidelines that would instruct future relational complications. How merciful of God to teach His people how be in holy relationship with Himself and one another? How kind and loving is He to teach them how to love Him well after all of the love He had lavished on them?

The book of Exodus continues with more detailed laws and also specifically prescribed ways to worship Yahweh. They had likely been exposed to some horrific and blasphemous methods of worship in Egypt, so God taught them how to properly worship Him. His intentions through the laws were good health, long life, holiness within the community as well as the individual, and proper worship. He said, "Worship the Lord your God, and his blessing will be on your food and water. I will take away sickness from among you, and none will miscarry or be barren in your land. I will give you a full life span" (Ex. 23:25-26). Imagine the global impact it would have had for the nations of the earth traveling through the promised land to witness this type of life in every follower of Yahweh. People from the ends of the earth would have been pounding down their doors to be a part of that!

Moses understood this. He said to the Lord, "If your Presence does not go with us, do not send us up from here. How will anyone know that you are pleased with me and with your people unless you go with us? What else will distinguish me and your people from all the other people on the face of the earth?" (Ex. 33:15-16). The Lord agreed that His presence would go with them, adding "I am making a covenant with you. Before all your people I will do wonders never before done in any nation in all the world. The people you live among will see how awesome is the work that I, the Lord, will do for you. Obey what I command you today" (Ex. 34:10). There was so much more at stake than the Israelites realized. It was through their obedience, holiness, and set-apartness that God would draw the nations back to Himself.

Unfortunately, Israel broke their very first wedding vow before they ever got to the honeymoon. While Moses was on the holy mountain obtaining the law from God, the people grew impatient with his absence and created the golden calves, even saying those idols were the gods who had brought them out of Egypt (Ex. 32:1-4). They were so quick to turn away from the One True God. The Lord burned with holy anger and was determined to destroy them all and start over with Moses (Ex. 32:9-10). But Moses pleaded on behalf of the people. He said, "Remember your servants Abraham, Isaac and Israel, to whom you swore by your own self: 'I will make your descendants as numerous as the stars in the sky and I will give your descendants all this land I promised them, and it will be their inheritance forever'" (Ex. 32:13). The Lord relented, for the sake of the covenant and His holy name.

Idolatry functionally puts God on the same level as everyone else. The whole purpose in all of this was to bring the world back into reconciled relationship with God. Idolatry, worshiping created things instead of the Creator, is particularly offensive to Yahweh. In giving the commandment not to make or bow down to idols, He said He is "a jealous God" and likened idolatry to hatred of God (Ex. 20:5-6). This would become a huge snare for the Israelites, as we will see. Through the prophet Isaiah, God would say, "I am the Lord; that is my name! I will not yield my glory to another or my praise to idols" (Is. 42:8). When Moses confronted the people for their atrocious sin, he did something quite interesting that can be easily overlooked. Scripture says Moses' anger burned at what he saw "and he took the calf they had made and burned it in the fire; then he ground it to a powder, scattered it on the water and made the Israelites drink it" (Ex. 32:20). The explanation of his actions does not come until Numbers chapter five, where the priests are instructed to sprinkle dust from the tabernacle floor into holy water, mixing it into a drink that carried a curse. It is called the test for an unfaithful wife (Num. 5:11-31). On the very spot where Yahweh had proposed His covenant to His beloved and they had consecrated themselves to Him, the newlywed Israel had already proven herself an unfaithful wife.

THE TABERNACLE

After the golden calf incident, the Lord told Moses to leave that place "and go up to the land [He] promised on oath to Abraham, Isaac and Jacob, saying, 'I will give it to your descendants'" (Ex. 33:1). He also said that He would send an angel in His place because He was not going to go with them, saying, "You are a stiff-necked people and I might destroy you on the way" (Ex. 33:3). That would become a regular moniker of His people, stiff-necked, which is another way of saying obstinate. Obstinate means "firmly or stubbornly adhering to one's purpose [or] opinion; not yielding to argument, persuasion, or entreaty."[11] The struggle to yield to the Lord's purpose for them was only beginning.

Thankfully, as we saw earlier, Moses did convince the Lord to have His presence go with them. However, the Presence of the Lord is a glory far beyond human comprehension or capacity. He said to Moses when asked to show him His glory, "You cannot see my face, for no one may see me and live" (Ex. 33:20). In the last few chapters of Exodus, the Lord gave specific instructions for how to build the ark of the covenant and the tabernacle. Skilled craftsmen from every walk of life were brought in on this project. They were to make a proper tabernacle for the Spirit of the Living God to dwell in their midst. It can certainly be tedious reading through chapters of specific measurements and details about the crafting of the ark and the tabernacle; however, these were vessels meant to carry the very Presence of a Holy God. It had to be perfect.

Moses inspected everything upon completion and found it had been done "just as the Lord had commanded" (Ex. 39:43). Everything was set up and consecrated to the Lord. Then, when everything was ready, the cloud of the Glory of the Lord came down upon the tent and filled the tabernacle (Ex. 40:34). Can you imagine the reverent awe that must have filled the camp as the Glory of the Lord came down? The cloud would rest over the tabernacle all day, lifting only when it was time for the Israelites to break down camp and move forward. At night, the holy fire of God

---

[11] "Obstinate," *Dictionary.com*, 2024, https://www.dictionary.com/browse/obstinate.

Chosen

would fill the cloud for all the Israelites to see (Ex. 40:36-38). Imagine what it must have been like for Israel to have a visible, tangible reminder of God's presence both day and night. Israel became a carrier of His Presence and His Glory for all the nations to see.

The Journey

LEVITICUS

The book of Leviticus contains much of what is called the Levitical law. Levi was one of the twelve sons of Jacob/Israel and each of those sons became a tribe of the Israelites (along with the half tribes of Ephraim and Manasseh, Joseph's sons). The tribe of Levi, or the Levites, were given the role of priests among the Israelites. Moses and his brother Aaron were Levites (Ex. 2:1) and Aaron had been chosen as the first priest (Ex. 28:1). Much of the book of Leviticus has to do with responsibilities of the priests, the Levites. It also contains laws that were specifically for the people of Israel. As Hamilton rightly states, "Leviticus summons Israel to a holy life," pointing out that the word "holy" occurs more in Leviticus than any other book of the Bible.[12]

Recalling the earlier discussion about the law as a gift, I want to offer a bit more evidence of that from Leviticus. Today, Christians will harp on being so grateful that they are no longer under the heavy yoke of the Levitical law. Most modern Jews do not even attempt to maintain the kosher lifestyle laid out in the Pentateuch. Having to keep up with and maintain over 600 laws on dietary restrictions, lifestyle choices, ways of worship, and sacrificial atonement requirements sounds impossible. It is important to keep in mind, however, that the goal was holiness for the community that would become a light for the nations. Furthermore, modern science confirms that many of the dietary and sanitation laws were way ahead of science and would

---

[12] Hamilton, *Handbook on the Pentateuch*, 232.

have led to a noticeably healthier lifestyle for the Israelites compared to the surrounding nations.

For example, there are multiple sections of Leviticus that deal with defiling skin diseases. Today, if someone were to show you a weird rash on their skin, you would know better than to touch it because you have the benefit of at least a basic understanding of the scientific phenomenon of contagion. That was not the case back then. When the Israelites came out of Egypt, God said that He would protect them from diseases that the Egyptians were not protected from (Ex. 15:26). There was certainly a supernatural protection here, but there was also a very different understanding of how disease worked in ancient Egypt. In that day, if one was struck with a defiling skin disease, they would have been more likely to believe it was a curse from an angry god than the result of touching an infected person and having it spread. God was imparting some level of knowledge and understanding of disease that science would not be able to confirm for generations to come.

Another example is found in the dietary restrictions. Keeping kosher means to abstain from unclean foods, like pork and shellfish. It also means following other rules like not consuming meat alongside dairy or meat containing blood. Again, many of these laws actually kept Israel in a noticeably healthier lifestyle than the surrounding nations. In a book called *The Maker's Diet* by Jordan S. Rubin, Rubin explores scientifically why the Levitical dietary laws are scientifically proven to lead to better holistic health. He says, "All of God's laws are like His law of gravity — they can't be changed. Our Creator specifically designed us to function best on The Maker's diet. In order to benefit from His plan, we must examine exactly which foods are unclean, unhealthy, or unacceptable according to both God and science."[13] God designed and created our bodies. Why would He not have unique insight into what makes our bodies function properly?

The point is not to convince you to begin eating or living according to Levitical law. The point is merely to highlight how the law was truly a gift to His people. Ultimately, it was about holiness for Israel, both ritually and morally. Living according to God's law would have drawn the attention of the nations as they witnessed the unique lifestyle of the Israelites. At the end of Leviticus, God laid out His specific reward for obedience. He told His people that if they followed His commands, He

---

[13] Jordan S. Rubin, *The Maker's Diet* (Shippensburg, PA: Destiny Image Publishers, 2005).

would bless the land, the coming of the rain, and the abundance of their crops (Lev. 26:3-5). He also said they would live in peace and safety in their land (Lev. 26:5-8). Best of all, He told them that He would keep His covenant with them, He would put His dwelling place among them, He would walk with them, and He would be their God (Lev. 26:9-12). It was not quite the Garden of Eden from Genesis one and two, but it would be as close as anyone had ever seen since then.

However, on the flip side of this promise of reward was His punishment for disobedience. Reading the rest of chapter twenty-six highlights all that entailed, and it was brutal. There would be "sudden terror [and] wasting diseases" (Lev. 26:16). God would set His face against theirs when they were confronted by their enemies (Lev. 26:17). Their sins would be punished "seven times over" (Lev. 26:18). He said, "Your strength will be spent in vain, because your soil will not yield its crop" (Lev. 26:20). Afflictions, plagues, famine, wild beasts that devour children, cannibalism, their land turned to a wasteland, and their people scattered among the nations. How could a good, loving, merciful God be so intense in the brutality of His punishment, especially toward His own people? It is important to remember that the laws were about giving the Israelite community access to the presence of a holy God. Their unholiness was a big deal because God's holiness was and is a big deal. God, wanting to dwell with His people, would of course respond dramatically when they did anything that would separate them from Himself.

Furthermore, they were going to be a city on a hill that could not be hidden. They would be on center stage for the entire world, representing Yahweh for all those far from Him so that ultimately other nations could dwell with God as well. He was refining them, making them pure and holy, for the sake of His name and His holy purpose:

> For my own name's sake I delay my wrath; for the sake of my praise I hold it back from you, so as not to destroy you completely. See, I have refined you, though not as silver; I have tested you in the furnace of affliction. For my own sake, for my own sake, I do this. How can I let myself by defamed? I will not yield my glory to another (Is. 48:9-11).

Yahweh is certainly "slow to anger" (Ex. 34:6). However, He will not allow His name to be defamed (Third commandment, Ex. 20:7) and He will not yield His glory to idols (First and second commandment, Ex. 20:3-6). This would be especially important among the nations meant to be reconciled with Him. "Yet in spite of this, when they are in the land of their enemies, I will not reject them or abhor them so as to destroy them completely, breaking my covenant with them" (Lev. 26:44). Slow to anger and also "abounding in love and faithfulness" (Ex. 34:6). He would punish them for disobedience, but He would never break the covenant.

WANDERING

I have yet to find a person who says that the book of Numbers is their favorite book in the Bible. It is understandable, as it starts out reading like a phonebook (for Gen Z and younger, a phonebook was this hugely thick book of yesteryear that had phone numbers and addresses of every person and business in the community. It was how we found people before the Internet). The rest of the book of Numbers contains more detailed laws and worship practices, along with a few stories from the Israelites time in the wilderness.

Although it may not be the most riveting read in the Old Testament, it is still quite important. The first few chapters that list out by name the different clans and how many people were in each clan might not contain much spiritual insight, but it shows the historicity of the story of the nation of Israel. These were actual people who left Egypt and followed Moses through the wilderness. These were actual events that happened. Good writers know that you do not include boring content in a story unless it is absolutely necessary. If the story of Israel were fictitious, nobody would go through the trouble of making up all of those names and numbers because most people do not want to read all of that anyway. However, the next time you do a Bible reading plan that brings you through the book of Numbers, remind yourself that the lists of names attest to the fact that these events actually happened. These people actually existed, and this story is actually true.

The Israelites finally arrived at the land of Canaan, the promised land. The Lord told Moses, "Send some men to explore the land of Canaan, which I am giving to the Israelites" (Num. 13:1). Twelve men went into the land and explored for forty days. They found the land pleasing and abundant, just as the Lord had said. However, ten of the twelve reported back that "the people who live there are powerful, and the cities are fortified and very large" (Num. 13:28). Only two men believed that the

Lord could deliver the land into their hands: Caleb and Joshua.

Joshua, son of Nun, was of the tribe of Ephraim (Num. 13:8). Caleb, son of Jephunneh, was of the tribe of Judah (Num. 13:6). However, there are multiple places in Scripture where Caleb is referred to as a Kenizzite (Num. 32:12; Josh. 14:6, 14). Back in Genesis chapter fifteen, when God was cutting the covenant with Abraham, He told Abraham that his descendants would inherit the promised land. God described the land for its inhabitants at the time: "the land of the Kenites, Kenizzites, Kadmonites, Hitties, Perizzites, Rephaites, Amorites, Canaanites, Girgashites and Jebusites" (Gen. 15:19-20). So, although Caleb was said to be from the tribe of Judah, he was also descended from the original Gentile inhabitants of the promised land. Theories abound on the explanation for this, but the most reasonable one is that somewhere along the generational line, Caleb's family became grafted into the line of Judah. Perhaps his family had also become enslaved by Egypt at some point. Regardless of how and when, Caleb's Gentile family line intersected with the lineage of Judah.

Caleb and Joshua were the only two of the twelve spies who believed the Lord could do what He said He would do and give them the promised land. When the people rebelled and rallied behind the fearful ten, the Lord became angry once again with the obstinate mistrust of His people. He said, "As surely as I live and as surely as the glory of the Lord fills the whole earth, not one of those who saw my glory and the signs I performed in Egypt and in the wilderness but who disobeyed me and tested me ten times – not one of them will ever see the land I promised on oath to their ancestors" (Num. 14:21-23). Imagine seeing all that the Lord had done in Egypt and since then and *still* not believing He was able to do what He said! In this situation, the Israelites trusted in human wisdom over the Lord's wisdom. Furthermore, they only saw their circumstances through their own eyes and their own strength. They were not exactly a military, and they knew that they alone could not defeat any other army. In the same way that they could not have defeated the Egyptians. But God. God did not tell them to overpower the Canaanites and take the land. He told them over and over that He would *give* them the land.

If they were going to accomplish what the Lord would do through them, they would have to be willing and trusting vessels of His glory, goodness, and redemption. In their human strength, they were nearly worthless against the armies of

Canaan. In the same way, they would be worthless to God's redemption plan in their human strength. They had to learn to trust in Him, to rely on Him for all of their needs, and to wait upon His Presence at all times and in all ways. Only Joshua and Caleb would see the promised land. And Caleb, the Gentile, was commended by God in a special way. God said, "But because my servant Caleb has a different spirit and follows me wholeheartedly, I will bring him into the land he went to, and his descendants will inherit it" (Num. 14;24)

Because of the Israelites shallow faith, the Lord had them wander the desert for forty years, learning trust and obedience. These lessons would need to be passed down to their children because they would be the ones to enter the promised land. Without having witnessed firsthand the mighty works of God in the exodus, the next generation would need an even greater reliance on God to accomplish His will. Even Moses would lose the privilege of entering the land. Although he trusted the Lord explicitly and repeatedly saved the Israelites from His holy wrath, Moses himself would succumb to the frustration of dealing with the stiff-necked people of Israel. In a foolish act of annoyance with them, Moses failed to trust in God's instruction for how to bring forth water for the people. The Lord said, "Because you did not trust me enough to honor me as holy in the sight of the Israelites, you will not bring this community into the land I give them" (Num. 20:12). Holiness requires full and complete obedience and trust. God's people must be holy because He is holy, and they would be His light in a dark world.

HOMECOMING

The first generation of Israelites who had come out of Egypt knew only the land of their captors as home. They spent the rest of their lives wandering the wilderness in penance for their stiff-necked distrust of Yahweh. That generation would be remembered as the generation that could never fully step out of slave mentality into sonship. The second generation knew only the wilderness as their home. The cloud by day and the fire by night guiding them from one temporary place of rest to the next was all they knew as home. However, to them God would say, "You have made your way around this hill country long enough; now turn north" (Deut. 2:2). God had a permanent home for them in a good land where His presence would dwell among them. It was time for them to go home.

The land that had been home to Abraham, Isaac, and Jacob as foreigners would become theirs. God said, "See, I have *given* you this land. Go in and take possession of the land the Lord swore he would give to your fathers – to Abraham, Isaac and Jacob – and to their descendants after them" (Deut. 1:8, emphasis added). Many modern Christians have a hard time reconciling the brutality with which the Israelites conquered the land. After all, the land was occupied by many different nations and the Israelites went in as a powerful military force, killing and conquering through the leading of Yahweh. Furthermore, were they not on a mission to bring the nations back to God? How did this hostile takeover reconcile with a God whose name meant "compassionate and gracious…slow to anger, abounding in love and faithfulness?" (Ex. 34:5-7). How could the God who was determined to reconcile all nations to Himself through this people, telling them to love their neighbor as themselves (Lev. 19:18) and treat the foreigner among them as native-born (Lev. 19:33-34), be the same God that commanded them to annihilate the Canaanites and other inhabitants of the promised land?

One could go all the way back to Genesis chapter fifteen to begin to understand the answers to these questions. God had told Abraham that while the Israelites were enslaved in Egypt, the people living in Canaan, the Amorites, would eventually get to a place where their sin would reach "its full measure" (Gen. 15:16). Historical archeological discoveries have shed some light into what this may have looked like. Atrocities like child sacrifice, violence and rape in worship of false gods, and sexual immorality like that seen in Sodom and Gomorrah (Gen. 14, 18:16-19:38). Back in Exodus chapter twenty-three, God told the people that He would drive out their enemies from Canaan "little by little," until they had increased enough to take full possession of the land (Ex. 23:30). He warned them not to make covenants with them or their gods, and not to allow them to live in the land, for "they will cause [the Israelites] to sin against [God], because the worship of their gods [would] certainly be a snare" (Ex. 23:32-33). These were not merely sinners in need of a Savior. These nations were corrupt to the core, pure evil whose sin would be a snare to the people of God.

Remember, there was great strategic purpose in bringing this nation of priests to the promised land. When they were finally on the brink of entering the land, Moses said:

> See, I have taught you decrees and laws as the Lord my God commanded me, so that you may follow them in the land you are entering to take possession of it. Observe them carefully, for this will show your wisdom and understanding *to the nations*, who will hear about all these decrees and say, "Surely this great nation is a wise and understanding people." What other nation is so great as to have their gods near them the way the Lord our God is near us whenever we pray to him? And what other nation is so great as to have such righteous decrees and laws as this body of laws I am setting before you today? (Deut. 4:5-8, emphasis added)

The purpose was to have a holy people, a nation of priests, set apart and on display for the world to see. Furthermore, He said:

> It is not because of your righteousness or your integrity that you are going in to take possession of their land; but on account of the wickedness of these nations, the Lord your God will drive them out before you, to accomplish what he swore to your fathers, to Abraham, Isaac and Jacob. Understand, then, that it is not because of your righteousness that the Lord your God is giving you this good land to possess, for you are a stiff-necked people (Deut. 9:5-6).

They had done nothing to earn this land. In fact, they did not even *deserve* it based on their behavior. Yet, that is precisely the point. It was not a gift given out of merit. It was a strategic part of God's plan. The reasons they were taking possession of it were two-fold: because the occupying nations were wicked and to accomplish the promise made to the patriarchs to use their descendants to bless the entire world. God repeated these purposes multiple times so that there would be no confusion. They did nothing to earn this favor and blessing. Rather, they were chosen for a purpose.

God said that it would be important to teach these commands to their children and grandchildren so as not to forget (Deut. 4:9; 6:4-9; 7:4). He promised repeatedly that following His commands would lead to blessings and long life in the land (Deut. 4:1, 40; 5:33; 6:3, 18, 24-25). He said:

> Has anything so great as this ever happened, or has anything like it ever been heard of? Has any other people heard the voice of God speaking out of fire, as you have, and lived? Has any god ever tried to take for himself one nation out of another nation, by testings, by signs and wonders, by war, by a mighty hand and an outstretched arm, or by great and awesome deeds, like all the things the Lord your God did for you in Egypt before your very eyes? You were shown these things so that you might know that the Lord is God; besides him there is no other (Deut. 4:32-35).

Much of Deuteronomy reads like an exhorting pep talk from Moses to the people. Please keep God's commands. Please stay holy. Please stay faithful. Do not forget the Lord and it will go so well for you in this land. "For you are a people holy to the Lord your God. The Lord your God has chosen you out of all the peoples on the face of the earth to be his people, his treasured possession" (Deut. 7:6). Simply love Him and obey Him, and His blessing will be poured over you and your families and overflow to the nations of the earth. "And now, Israel, what does the Lord your God ask of you but to fear the Lord your God, to walk in obedience to him, to love him, to serve the Lord your God with all your heart and with all your soul, and to observe the Lord's commands and decrees that I am giving you today *for your own good?*" (Deut. 10:12-13, emphasis added). The law and the covenant were for their good and for His glory, and Moses was begging them not to forget that.

This was perhaps the greatest covenantal agreement that has ever existed. All of God's commands could be summarized as "to love the Lord your God, to walk in obedience to him and to hold fast to him" (Deut. 11:22). In response, He promised them long and good life in a good and abundant land, protection from diseases and victory over their enemies, and best of all, His Presence. All of His commands and decrees were for their good and for His glory. "And the Lord has declared this day that you are his people, his treasured possession as he promised, and that you are to keep all his commands. He has declared that he will set you in praise, fame and honor high above all the nations he had made and that you will be a people holy to the Lord your God" (Deut. 26:18-19). This was His great redemption plan for the whole earth.

The blessings that would come as a result of their obedience are shown in Deuteronomy 28:1-14, while the curses for disobedience were shown in verses 15-68. The punishment would be more severe because as much as their obedience and blessing would be on center stage for all the nations to see, so would their disobedience. Among the various harsh curses that they could expect for disobedience, one of the worst would be losing their land. God said that He would "scatter [them] among the nations, from one end of the earth to the other," to lands where they would feel no peace or rest, only anxiety and despair (Deut. 28:64-66). However, God promised to always be a God willing to accept their repentance. He said:

> **When all these blessings and curses I have set before you come on you and you take them to heart wherever the Lord your God disperses you among the nations, and when you and your children return to the Lord your God and obey him with all your heart and with all your soul according to everything I command you today, then the Lord your God will restore your fortunes and have compassion on you and gather you again from all the nations where he scattered you. Even if you have been banished to the most distant land under the heavens, from there the Lord your God will gather you and bring you back. He will bring you to the land that belonged to your ancestors, and you will take possession of it (Deut. 30:1-5).**

Throughout the book of Deuteronomy, Moses kept reiterating the same exhortation. Israel, you have the choice to live in His blessing and favor, or to choose the path of death. He begged them to choose life (Deut. 30:19-20).

As the story in the promised land played out, we see that they did not often choose the path of life. They would become a nation trapped in a cycle of rebellion and sin, and then shame and repentance. But of course, this did not surprise God. He told Moses, "You are going to rest with your ancestors, and these people will soon prostitute themselves to foreign gods of the land they are entering. They will forsake me and break the covenant I made with them" (Deut. 31:16). Then He gave Moses a song to recite for the people that would predict their rebellion and betrayal. I would encourage you to pause, set down this book, and read the song that God gave Moses in Deuteronomy chapter thirty-two. The song is as poetic as it is prophetic. In it, God showed His merciful choosing and unmerited love and favor of Israel. However, He highlighted that they would repay him with brazen, unashamed infidelity. His love for them, analogized like that of a mother and also that of a faithful husband, would be met only with arrogant entitlement. Were it not for the sake of His Holy Name, He would have wiped them from the face of the earth entirely. He said that He would "make them envious by those who are not a people," another nation that would rejoice for Him (Deut. 32:21, 43). Almost two thousand years later, the apostle Paul would quote these verses in his letter to a Gentile church in Rome. But we will have to walk through a bit more of Israel's story to fully understand what Paul meant.

STRONG AND COURAGEOUS

Joshua, son of Nun, was chosen as Moses' successor. He and Caleb were the only two from the initial exodus generation that were allowed to enter the promised land because of their unwavering faith in God's protection and provision. His story, shown in the book bearing his name, starts with God exhorting him to be strong and courageous three times (Josh. 1:6, 7, 9). God's presence would go with him, so he had nothing to fear.

The Israelites entered the promised land by way of the parted Jordan River. Their journey from slavery to sonship was bookended by two miraculous crossings through water. The imagery of baptism is easy to see. The Israelites went into the Red Sea as slaves on the run from a tyrannical master. They came out as a nation set free and chosen by God. Forty years later, they went into the Jordan River as wandering nomads. They came out as more than conquerors, stepping foot into their new homeland. "He did this so that all the peoples of the earth might know that the hand of the Lord is powerful and so that [they] might always fear [Him]" (Josh. 4:24). Although God had made it abundantly clear that they were to "destroy with the sword every living thing" (Josh. 6:21) in Jericho, God showed His mercy upon those who earnestly called out to Him, like Rahab and her family.

The book of Joshua shows the conquering of the land through the miraculous presence and protection of the Lord. They had become a mighty people with more military experience than they had possessed in Egypt; however, the conquering of the land was intentionally not to be credited to their might or prowess. God intervened in ways that showed the nations that He was the God of all gods. As an example, in chapter ten the battle was won because the Lord delayed the sun going down by an entire day and "hurled large hailstones down" on their enemy (Josh. 10:1-15, 11). They really could not take credit for that victory in their own strength. The Lord continued to lead them in conquering the land of their enemies. "Surely the Lord was fighting for Israel!" (Josh. 10:14).

Joshua's life was characterized by one military conquest after another. His life attests to his courage and strength, both of which came from his faith in God. At the end of his life, following the model of Moses, he gave Israel a reminder history lesson of everything the Lord had done for them and an exhortation to keep the covenant (Josh. 23 – 24). Reminiscent of when God had proposed His covenant to His people at the foot of Mount Sinai, the people were given a choice as to whether or not they wanted to enter into the covenant. Joshua said, "But if serving the Lord seems undesirable to you, then choose for yourselves this day whom you will serve, whether the gods your ancestors served beyond the Euphrates, or the gods of the Amorites, in whose land you are living. But as for me and my household, we will serve the Lord" (Josh. 24:15). Once again, Israel said yes.

> **Far be it from us to forsake the Lord to serve other gods! It was the Lord our God himself who brought us and our parents up out of Egypt, from that land of slavery, and performed those great signs before our eyes. He protected us on our entire journey and among all the nations through which we traveled. And the Lord drove out before us all the nations, including the Amorites, who lived in the land. We too will serve the Lord, because he is our God (Deut. 24:16-18).**

Then, as if to ask if they were really sure about the commitment they were making, Joshua said, "You are not able to serve the Lord, he is a holy God; he is a jealous God. He will not forgive your rebellion and your sins. If you forsake the Lord and serve foreign gods, he will turn and bring disaster on you and make an end of you, after he has been good to you" (Deut. 24:19-20). Yet, Israel insisted upon her devotion, saying, "No! We will serve the Lord" (Deut. 24:21). Then Joshua said, "You are witnesses against yourselves that you have chosen to serve the Lord," to which they replied, "Yes, we are witnesses" (Deut. 24:22). Israel had conquered the land and the covenant had been confirmed. Now would be their time to shine the light of Yahweh to the nations.

THE PERIOD OF THE JUDGES

At a place called Bokim, which means "weepers," the Israelites made one of their most costly choices in the promised land. Judges 1:27-36 shows that many of the tribes of Israel did not drive out the people completely, but rather, pressed some into forced labor or allowed some to live among them. The Lord had warned His people about this, but they disregarded His instruction. At Bokim, an angel of the Lord appeared, reminding them that the Lord had said "I will never break my covenant with you, and you shall not make a covenant with the people of this land … they will become traps for you, and their gods will become snares to you" (Judg. 2:1-3). When Israel did not obey God's command to destroy the inhabitants of the land, God said He would not drive them out but rather, would use them "to test Israel and see whether they [would] keep the way of the Lord and walk in it as their ancestors did" (Judg. 2:22). Israel had missed the opportunity to be rid of the people that would become a trap and a snare. Throughout the rest of their history that is exactly what happened. Instead of being a light to the nations, they became influenced and ensnared by them and their wicked ways.

Scripture immediately shows the beginning of the cycle of disobedience and defeat. Soon there was an entire generation who had grown up knowing "neither the Lord nor what he had done for Israel" (Judg. 2:10). They had forgotten Him and therefore had forsaken Him. So, God gave them over to their enemies (Judg. 2:11-15). Without His presence, they were no longer able to overpower their enemies in battle. However, just as He had promised, God did not forget His people, nor did He let His anger burn forever. God raised up judges to save them, but they did not listen to them (Judg. 2:16-17). "Unlike their ancestors, they quickly turned from following the ways of their ancestors, the way of obedience to the Lord's command" (Judg. 2:17). God would raise up a judge, they would experience a temporary reprieve from their enemies, but then upon the death of the judge, they would return to "ways even more corrupt than those of their ancestors" (Judg. 2:19).

Each generation grew worse and worse. The judges themselves grew more corrupt. Gideon, as an example, grew from a cowardly nobody to a hero in Israel when the Lord called him to lead an army against the Midianites (Judg. 6 – 7). "During Gideon's lifetime, the land had peace forty years" (Judg. 8:28). However, at the end of his lifetime, he also turned away from the Lord. The people asked him to rule over them and he said that he would not, nor would his son, because the Lord would rule over them (Judg. 8:22-23). These certainly sound like the words of a righteous man. He then asked each of them to give him one gold earring from their shares of plunder (Judg. 8:24). He received roughly the equivalent of over 43 pounds of gold from this request. He then took the gold, melted it down, and made an ephod (Judg. 8:27). An ephod is a breastplate worn by the priests. However, this ephod would not become part of any priestly garment. Gideon put it on display in his hometown as an idol and "all Israel prostituted themselves by worshiping it there" (Judg. 8:27). That part of the story never seems to end up in any children's Bible stories on heroes of the faith.

The period of the judges was a dark time in Israel's history. There were some stories of triumph and repentance, as God was still operating in their midst, even in times of rebellion. But overall, the nation sank deeper and deeper into sin and idolatry. They could not resist the allure of the wickedness of the other nations that surrounded them. Repeatedly, the book of Judges points out the fact that "in those days Israel had no king" (Judg. 18:1, 19:1, 21:25). God did not want a monarchy for His people. He wanted a theocracy for His people. He wanted to be their God *and* their King. But like a stubborn, obstinate child, they refused to listen. A fitting end to a tragic period, the book of Judges ends with the statement "In those days Israel had no king; everyone did as they saw fit" (Judg. 21:25).

Summary

Up until this point, we have gone through each book of the Old Testament in the order in which they appear in the Bible. As has been said, however, the intention of this book is not to become a commentary on the whole Bible. Rather, the intention is to show the purpose of Israel. At this point, a summary seems fitting. God created humankind for relationship with Himself, and His desire was to fill the earth with those who bore His image and reflected His glory. While mankind broke that relationship when they chose willful sin and disobedience, God's desire never changed. He still wanted that relationship, not because He needed it, but because He always has been a good Father.

As mankind wallowed in the consequences of our own sinful choices, God began implementing a redemption plan. He would bring about relational reconciliation through the descendants of one man. This man, who would become known as Abraham, was a righteous man, though certainly not without sin. It was his belief and trust in God that made him eligible to be used as an instrument of redemption. God made a promise to him that through his offspring, all peoples on earth would be blessed with a reconciled relationship with God. Those offspring would become known as the nation of Israel.

Israel was chosen to be a nation set apart from the world for the purpose of reconciling the world back to God. His blessing and favor would be upon them so noticeably that they would become a beacon of hope in a dark and broken world. God would set them in the center of the nations and use them to draw all peoples back to Himself. Unfortunately, living up to their name, which means "he who struggles with God," the nation of Israel would struggle to keep their end of the covenant. Their faithfulness to God and His covenant was constantly being tested and they were constantly unfaithful.

The next part in the story will be Israel's history in the promised land throughout the Old Testament. For the sake of gaining clarity, in the order in which they appear in the Bible the books of Joshua through Esther tell the story of Israel's history. The books of Job through Song of Solomon are considered the poetic books of the Old Testament, though they also contain some elements of Israelite history. Then, the final books of the Old Testament, Isaiah through Malachi, are the books of the prophets. The prophets came throughout Israel's history with words from the Lord. Moses had told the people before they entered the promised land that they were not permitted to practice sorcery or divination as a way of understanding God's will for them (Deut. 18:14). Instead, Moses said, "The Lord your God will raise up for you a prophet like me from among you, from your own people. You must listen to him ... [God said] I will put my words in his mouth. He will tell them everything I command him. I myself will call to account anyone who does not listen to my words that the prophet speaks in my name" (Deut.18:15-20). History would prove that the Israelites would have just as hard a time listening to the prophets as they had listening to Moses.

Understanding the Historical Arrangement in the OT

Going chronologically through the Old Testament, we now get to the history of the nation of Israel in the promised land. The story of Ruth should be chronologically next, but I want to put her story off until later for reasons I will explain. In his book *Handbook on the Historical Books*, Victor P. Hamilton aptly states, "There is no shortage of books dealing with this period of biblical Israel."[14] Indeed, I will not be able to do this topic justice in the eyes of many. I am not a historian, nor do I claim to be an expert on ancient or modern Israel. However, biblical illiteracy and the rampant belief in American churches that the Old Testament is irrelevant to today's Christian has left most modern Christians unaware of even the most basic history of Israel. The problem with that is that it is impossible to understand the mission and role of the Church without understanding the mission and history of God's chosen people. This will not be a deep dive into the nuances of their history, but rather, a high-level overview that traces the Abrahamic Covenant from Abraham, all the way through the history of God's chosen people, until it intersects with your life today.

The books of the Bible are not ordered chronologically, though some of them work out that way. When it comes to the historical parts, there is a lot of overlap between

---

[14] Victor P. Hamilton, *Handbook on the Historical Books: Joshua, Judges, Ruth, Samuel, Kings, Chronicles, Ezra-Nehemiah, Esther* (Grand Rapids, MI: Baker Academic, 2001), 13.

the books. Perhaps a chart would be helpful in visually understanding.

		JOEL	
		MICAH	
		ISAIAH	
		ZEPHANIAH	JONAH
	AMOS	HABAKKUK	NAHUM
	HOSEA	JEREMIAH	OBADIAH
1 SAMUEL	2 SAMUEL	1 KINGS	2 KINGS
	1 CHRONICLES	2 CHRONICLES	
	PSALMS	PROVERBS	
		ECCLESIASTES	
		SONG OF SOLOMON	

C. 1120 B.C.   C. 605 B.C.

The history of Israel after the period of the judges (which lasted about 300 years) until the time that Israel was exiled from the land (a topic for the next section) spanned from about 1120 B.C. to about 605 B.C., roughly 515 years. The two books of Samuel and the two books of Kings tell the story sort of as it was happening, whereas Chronicles was more of a later reflection back on the history for post-exilic Jews who might not have known their history. Some have suggested that the two variations reflect the difference between an optimistic versus realistic view of the history. Others have suggested one views more the spiritual or religious side of the history whereas the other is more the political or secular side of the people's history. Regardless, 1 and 2 Samuel and 1 and 2 Kings tell one continuous story, and 1 and 2 Chronicles retell that story. It is similar to the way that the four gospel accounts tell the same story, but with varying differences in voice, perspective, and audience.

Many of the other books find their place within that historical narrative. For example, many of the psalms were written by David, which would have historically taken place in 2 Samuel. Many of the proverbs, along with the books of Ecclesiastes and Song of Solomon, were written by Solomon, which would have historically taken place in 1 Kings. Furthermore, the prophets were sent to deliver messages from God to His people throughout their history. Although canonically all the books of poetry/literature are placed together (after the historical books) and all of the books of prophecy are placed together (at the end of the Old Testament), chronologically they would have been mixed within the history of the Israelites.

The History

SAMUEL, THE PROPHET PRIEST

First Samuel begins with the heartfelt cries of a barren woman who was begging the Lord for a child. Hannah's faith brought forth Samuel, who would become one of Israel's greatest prophets. The boy, Samuel, "continued to grow in stature and in favor with the Lord and with people" (1 Sam. 2:26).[15] As he grew, he served under a priest named Eli. Eli's sons were "scoundrels," sleeping with women in what would be equivalent to today's church lobby and taking the good parts of the meat given as sacrifices to Yahweh for themselves, which was absolutely forbidden (1 Sam. 2:12-25). God told Eli that his family's days as priests were numbered because of their wickedness (1 Sam. 2:27-36). "In those days the word of the Lord was rare; there were not many visions" (1 Sam. 3:1). Under Eli's spiritual leadership, Israel was certainly not thriving.

God raised up Samuel as a prophet and priest under Eli. During this transitional time, the ark of God was stolen by Philistine raiders and the glory of the Lord departed with it for seven months (1 Sam. 6:1). In that time period, God brought destruction, sickness, devastation, and confusion upon the Philistines, even bringing the idol of their god onto his face before the ark (1 Sam. 5:4). Eventually it was returned to Israel, though not because Israel went after it. Rather, God orchestrated

---

[15] The same was said of Jesus in Luke 2:52

The History

its return on the back of a cow-drawn wagon (1 Sam. 6). The Philistines were one of the nations that Israel was supposed to have destroyed when conquering the land. However, because the Israelites did not follow the Lord's instructions, the Philistines plagued the Israelites for centuries. Samuel, a man of God, rallied the people together, calling them to abandon their worthless idols and return to the Lord once again. They did and he was able to lead them in a powerful (though not complete) victory against the Philistines.

Samuel was a good leader in Israel, the likes of which they had not seen in quite some time. When he was advanced in age, however, the people said, "You are old, and your sons do not follow your ways; now appoint a king to lead us, such as all the other nations have" (1 Sam. 8:5). They had never had a king in Israel; God wanted to be their King. The request displeased Samuel, but he prayed to the Lord on their behalf. God said, "Listen to all that the people are saying to you; it is not you they have rejected, but they have rejected me as their king. As they have done from the day I brought them up out of Egypt until this day, forsaking me and serving other gods, so they are doing to you" (1 Sam. 8:7-8). Since the exodus, God had been trying to set them apart as a light to the nations. Instead, they chose time and time again to become just like all the other nations.

Samuel warned them of the consequences of appointing a king, per the Lord's instructions. Any king chosen would reign over them and claim his rights as a king (1 Sam. 8:9-18). Yet, the people would not be deterred from their request. They said, "We want a king over us. Then we will be like all the other nations, with a king to lead us and go out before us and fight our battles" (1 Sam. 8:19-20). When reading the history from the books of Joshua, Judges, 1 & 2 Samuel, and 1 & 2 Kings, we can easily see that when the people kept their part of the covenant and followed the Lord's commands and decrees, He was the one who led them victoriously in battle. He was the one who fought on their behalf and kept their enemies far from them. The reasons they were constantly being defeated by their enemies were all direct consequences of their own choices, not their lack of an earthly king! The Philistines would not have even been an issue had the Israelites destroyed them in the first place as they had been commanded. God had given them Jericho not through military might, but through His Presence. The victory was theirs only because it was His. Yet, here they were, believing that the victories would once again be theirs if only they had an earthly king, just like the nations that were regularly coming against them.

Imagine how this must have grieved the heart of God. Like a stubborn, obstinate child, His people thought they knew better. Parents know that sometimes, as hard as it is, we have to let our children learn lessons the hard way. Hamilton states, "God does not overrule the people and veto their request, their questionable motives withstanding. Nor does he withdraw into indifference, exasperated because it hasn't been done his way. Rather, he uses the realities of the moment, and in all things he works for good."[16] Their obstinate request was not a surprise to God, who had long ago anticipated this and made provisions in the law for a king. Way back in Deuteronomy seventeen, about 300 years prior to this, God had said through Moses, "When you enter the land the Lord your God is giving you and have taken possession of it and settled in it, and you say, 'Let us set a king over us like all the nations around us,' be sure to appoint over you the king the Lord your God choses. He must be from among your own people" (Deut. 17:14-15). He also included stipulations back then to keep the king from excesses and to keep him in alignment with the Lord (Deut. 14-20). God wanted to be their King, but they rejected Him as King.

SAUL, THE PEOPLE'S KING

Thus, the Lord gave Israel her first king, the strikingly tall and handsome Saul (1 Sam. 9:1). Samuel anointed Saul as ruler of God's people (1 Sam. 10:1) and "the Spirit of God came on him in power" and he began prophesying (1 Sam. 10:10). Samuel said to the people:

> Now here is the king you have chosen, the one you asked for; see, the Lord has set a king over you. If you fear the Lord and serve and obey him and do not rebel against his commands, and if both you and the king who reigns over you follow the Lord your God—good! But if you do not obey the Lord, and if you rebel against his commands, his hand will be against you, as it was against your ancestors ... Do not be afraid ... You have done all this evil; yet do not turn away from the Lord, but serve the Lord

---

[16] Hamilton, *Handbook on the Historical Books*, 231.

with all your heart. Do not turn away after useless idols. They can do you no good, nor can they rescue you, because they are useless. *For the sake of his great name* the Lord will not reject his people, because the Lord was pleased to make you his own (1 Sam. 12:13-15, 20-22, emphasis added).

Despite their rejection of God as king, God was still intent on using them to accomplish what had been promised to the patriarchs. God would still use this people to bless all peoples on earth and reconcile humanity back to Himself. "For the sake of his great name" God would keep His promises and uphold His covenants.

Unfortunately, it did not take long for Saul to lose the favor and blessing of the Lord. In chapter thirteen, the Israelites were once again in a battle with the Philistines. The intention was to make a sacrifice to the Lord before the battle began, but Samuel was late in arriving. As the priest, he was the only one God approved for making such sacrifices. As humans often do, Saul lost patience and took matters into his own hands. Saul made the sacrifice to the Lord and just as he was finishing, Samuel arrived (1 Sam. 13:10). There was no justification for what Saul had done. He had been anointed as king, not as priest. He did not follow the Lord's commands. Samuel rebuked him harshly, saying, "You have done a foolish thing … you have not kept the command the Lord your God gave you; if you had, he would have established your kingdom over Israel for all time. But now your kingdom will not endure; the Lord has sought out a man after his own heart and appointed him ruler of his people, because you have not kept the Lord's command" (1 Sam. 13:13-14). Saul's impatience led to his downfall as king of Israel.

The Lord rejected Saul as king (1 Sam. 15:26) and instead chose David, telling Samuel, "Do not consider his appearance or his height…The Lord does not look at the things human beings look at. People look at the outward appearance, but the Lord looks at the heart" (1 Sam. 16:7). David was anointed and filled with the power of the Spirit of God (1 Sam. 16:13). He would become Israel's greatest earthly king. Though he was far from perfect, he was said to be a man after God's own heart. He was not the strikingly handsome, tall, regal type of king, nor was he (at first) a powerful military leader. He was a shepherd, a musician, and a poet. He was one who would worship the Lord with reckless abandon (2 Sam. 6:16-22) and one who would care for the flock of Israel. He waited nearly fifteen years from when he was anointed king to when he actually took the throne, during which time he spent much of it running for his life from Saul. Multiple times he had the opportunity to kill Saul, but he would not dare do such a thing to the Lord's anointed (1 Sam 26:9-11). David trusted God and His perfect timing.

DAVID, THE SHEPHERD KING

Many of David's stories are well-known, even among the most biblically unfamiliar crowds. However, for the sake of the purpose of this book, I want to revisit some. First is probably the most famous story of his, known by children and known colloquially by even the non-religious: David and Goliath. David had been anointed king, but was still many years from the throne. Furthermore, he was merely a boy and the youngest of his father's eight sons. One day, David was sent on an errand to bring lunch to his older brothers who were fighting the Philistines alongside Saul's men (1 Sam. 17:12-19). As the familiar part of the story goes, he arrived to find all the militia afraid of an oversized Philistine warrior. Saul had offered wealth and his daughter's hand in marriage to whichever man could defeat Goliath, yet none dared. David might have been compelled by the money or the royal bride like most men were, but he was also appalled at the way Goliath disgraced God's people Israel and defied "the armies of the living God" (1 Sam. 17:26). He stepped forward courageously (though in all appearance foolishly) to fight the Philistine champion.

Before the fight began, David and Goliath began a typical exchange of derogatory remarks and bold threats, otherwise known today as trash talking. David said:

> You come against me with sword and spear and javelin, but I come against you in the name of the Lord Almighty, the God of the armies of Israel, whom you have defied. This day the Lord will deliver you into my hands, and I'll strike you down and cut off your head. This very day I will give the carcasses of the Philistine army to the birds and the wild animals, *and the whole world will know that there is a God in Israel* (1 Sam. 17:45-46, emphasis added).

Perhaps you have read this story more times than you could count, in cartoon version, devotional style, and everything in between. Regardless, please do not miss this. David said, "The whole world will know that there is a God in Israel" (v.46).

The whole world! David knew that there was more at stake here than this battle alone. There was more at stake here than the promised wealth, the princess bride, and even his own anointing and calling as king. David declared prophetically that the whole purpose in this was so that the whole world would know the God of Israel. God's glory among the nations was what was really at stake. The entire purpose for which Israel had been chosen had now been declared by the king after God's own heart.

Hamilton makes a very astute observation. In 1 Samuel 8:22, God told Samuel to "give them a king." Give Israel *their* king. However, in verse 16:1, He says, "I have provided for myself a king" (ESV). As Hamilton says, "Saul is the king appointed for the people…but David is the king appointed for God."[17] David became the king who was loved by "all Israel and Judah" (1 Sam. 18:16). His life story would go on to include murder, sexual immorality, lying, deceit, and a failure to lead his children in the ways of the Lord. Yet, God still used David in mighty ways. His life would bear testimony to the fact that "The Lord rewards every man for his righteousness and faithfulness" (1 Sam. 26:23).

David understood, at least to some extent, Israel's calling as a light for God to the Gentile nations. He wrote about it prophetically in his psalms to the Lord. First Chronicles chapter sixteen records one that is also recorded in Psalms 96 and 105. It says:

> Give praise to the Lord, call on his name; *make known among the nations* what he has done … Remember the wonders he has done, his miracles, and the judgments he pronounced, you his servants, the descendants of Israel, his chosen ones, the children of Jacob. He is the Lord our God; his judgments are in all the earth. He remembers his covenant forever, the promise he made, for a thousand generations, *the covenant he made with Abraham*, the oath he swore to Isaac. He confirmed it to Jacob as a decree, to Israel as an everlasting covenant … sing to the Lord, all the earth; proclaim his salvation day after day. *Declare his glory among the nations*, his marvelous deeds among all peoples … Ascribe to the Lord, all you families of nations, ascribe to the Lord

---

[17] Hamilton, *Handbook on the Historical Books*, 254.

glory and strength. Ascribe to the Lord the glory due his name; bring an offering and come before him ... Let the heavens rejoice, let the earth be glad; let them say among the nations, "The Lord reigns!" (1 Chron. 16:8-31, emphasis added)

David became king of Israel at age thirty and reigned for forty years (2 Sam. 5:4). He conquered Jerusalem, which he called "the City of David," and "he became more and more powerful, because the Lord God Almighty was with him (2 Sam. 5:6-10). David knew "that the Lord had established him as king over Israel and had exalted his kingdom for the sake of his people Israel" (2 Sam. 5:12). David's kingdom was established for the sake of the Israelites. The Israelites had been established for the sake of God's glory, to become a "nation of priests" (Ex. 19:5-6) and a light to the gentiles (Is. 49:6).

Furthermore, God would make some pretty exceptional promises to David. Reminiscent of God's promise to Abraham, He told David that He would make his name great, "like the names of the greatest men on earth" (2 Sam. 7:9; 1 Chron. 17:8). He also promised David, "I will raise up your offspring to succeed you, who will come from your own body, and I will establish his kingdom" (2 Sam. 7:12; 1 Chron. 17:11). Again, the promise reverberates from history, echoing words spoken by God over Abraham, Isaac, and Jacob. And just like His promise to them, God's promise to make David's name great would point back to the name of Yahweh. Then, God told David that his son would build a "house for my Name" (2 Sam. 7:13; 1 Chron. 17:12). David was ashamed that he lived in an immaculate palace while God's presence still resided in the ark in a tent. He vowed to build Him a proper house, but God said that was a job for his son, not him. Lastly, God told David, "Your house and your kingdom will endure forever before me; your throne will be established forever" (2 Sam. 7:15-16; 1 Chron. 17:12, 14). What an incredible promise.

The prophetic nature of these promises cannot be overstated. There would be immediate fulfillment and future fulfillment down David's generational line. In much the same way as the blessing would come to Abraham's son, Isaac, that blessing would also come to David's son, Solomon. Furthermore, in the same way that the blessing flowed *through* Isaac to future descendants, the blessing would flow through Solomon to future descendants. God's prophetic promises are rarely one dimensional. The picture it creates is like a long head of hair in a French braid. For those unfamiliar, the French braid is one that goes all the way down the back of one's head and beyond. It is done by grabbing three small sections of hair at the top of the head. One at a time, the side pieces are crossed over the middle piece. As the stylist continues down the back of the hair, another small section is gathered with the side piece before it is crossed over and incorporated into the original three. With each added piece, the braid grows, and the added pieces become so well incorporated that it becomes harder to distinguish which strands were part of the original and which were added along the way.

This is how the Abrahamic Covenant goes throughout all of Scripture. Each person, each story, each generation is another piece that is incorporated into the big picture. What began with Abraham, Isaac, and Jacob would eventually include every story in the Old Testament coming together to form one beautiful masterpiece.

David's response to the Lord's promises is exactly what one might expect from a man after God's own heart. He started by saying, "Who am I, Sovereign Lord, and what is my family that you have brought me this far? And as if this were not enough in your sight, Sovereign Lord, you have also spoken about the future of the house of your servant – and this decree, Sovereign Lord, is for a human being!" (2 Sam. 7:18-19) Had Abraham been as poetic as David, his response may have been similar. Then David said, "Do as you promised, *so that your name will be great forever*" (2 Sam. 7:25-26, emphasis added). David knew that he was unworthy of the blessings that God was promising. He knew that he did not deserve to simply be blessed without purpose. He recognized that the blessing carried a purpose. Just as when God told the Israelites that they were not gaining the land because of their own righteousness but rather they were gaining the land to accomplish the covenant God had established with the patriarchs, the blessing being given to David was the same. It had a purpose, and that purpose was to glorify God throughout the earth.

Don N. Howell, Jr. notes that "under David the borders of Israel expanded and, including the tributary nations brought under his control, the nation realized for the first time, at least temporarily, her promised domain (Gen. 15:18-21)."[18] David grew to be a mighty military leader, and a successful diplomat and politician. Howell goes on to say, "All of the treaties, tributes, and expanding boundaries brought to Israel

---

[18] Don N. Howell, Jr., *Servants of the Servant: A Biblical Theology of Leadership*, (Eugene, OR: Wipf & Stock Publishers, 2003), 91.

political security and sources of material abundance which would turn Israel from a divided, constricted tribal confederation to a united, growing prosperous nation."[19] Of course, David would be the first to recognize that these all came from Yahweh. He recognized God as the true source of blessing to him and to Israel.

Alongside the story of Goliath, the other story probably most well-known from David's life was not heroic but shows us that even a man after God's own heart falls vastly short of perfection. Unfortunately, his immense moral failure with Bathsheba became a huge part of his legacy. He broke four of the ten commandments in that one encounter (coveting, adultery, and eventually lying and murder). Although he confessed his sin from what seems to be a genuinely repentant heart (2 Sam. 12:13-17), the consequences of his sin would be calamity, discord, and death in his own family (vv.10-12). Despite this being one of the biggest marks against his godly character and the reason his story becomes increasingly tragic from that point on, David would still be remembered as Israel's greatest king. He was far from a perfect king, but as Howell says, "He is the exemplar of the theocratic ruler characterized by undivided devotion to the Lord and obedience to the covenant."[20]

SOLOMON, THE WISE KING

Solomon was the second child born to David through Bathsheba, the first one having died as a result of David's sin (2 Sam. 12:13-14). For reasons known only to the Lord, of all of David's sons, Solomon was the one chosen as the next king. Hamilton states that "only four Old Testament kings are divinely chosen (via a prophetic representative): (1) Saul; (2) David; (3) Jeroboam; (4) Jehu."[21] However, there is a passage that could be argued as God choosing Solomon. In 1 Chronicles chapter twenty-two, God told David that he could not be the one to build the temple because David had shed too much blood on the earth in all of Israel's military conquests (1 Chron. 22:8). Then the Lord said:

> You will have a son who will be a man of peace and rest, and I will give him rest from all his enemies on every side. His name will be Solomon, and I will grant Israel peace and quiet during

---

[19] Howell, *Servants of the Servant*, 91.
[20] Ibid., 101.
[21] Hamilton, *Handbook on the Historical Books*, 230.

his reign. He is the one who will build a house for my Name. He will be my son, and I will be his father. And I will establish the throne of his kingdom over Israel forever (1 Chron. 22:9-10).

Regardless of whether or not this shows that Solomon was divinely chosen as king, he was clearly chosen to be the son through which the covenant and the everlasting throne would be passed down.

Solomon became known as the wisest king and by many, the wisest man that ever lived because of a wise and godly request. The Lord appeared to him and told him to ask for whatever he wanted (1 Ki. 3:5). Solomon began his request by acknowledging how good the Lord had been to David "because he was faithful to you and righteous and upright in heart" (1 Ki. 3:6). Then Solomon admitted in humility that he needed the Lord's help to rule God's people; therefore, he asked for wisdom and a discerning heart (1 Ki. 3:7-9). God replied by giving him what he asked for, as well as what he did not ask for: wealth, honor, and wisdom unrivaled by any other king (1 Ki. 3:10-13).

God used that wisdom and fame not just for the benefit of Solomon and the nation of Israel, but more than that, He used it for His name's sake. Scripture says:

> God gave Solomon wisdom and very great insight, and a breadth of understanding as measureless as the sand on the seashore. Solomon's wisdom was greater than the wisdom of all the people of the East, and greater than all the wisdom of Egypt. He was wiser than anyone else, including Ethan the Ezrahite— wiser than Heman, Kalkol and Darda, the sons of Mahol. And *his fame spread to all the surrounding nations.* He spoke three thousand proverbs and his songs numbered a thousand and five. He spoke about plant life, from the cedar of Lebanon to the hyssop that grows out of walls. He also spoke about animals and birds, reptiles and fish. *From all nations people came to listen to Solomon's wisdom,* sent by all the kings of the world, who had heard of his wisdom (1 Ki. 4:29-34, emphasis added)..

Solomon was blessed with wisdom and God used that blessing to bless the nations. Furthermore, Solomon did end up building God a great temple to house His

Presence among His people. One of the neighboring kings, Hiram of Tyre, was commissioned by Solomon to bring in the great cedar trees of Lebanon for the project. In response, Hiram said, "Praise be to the Lord today, for he has given David a wise son to rule over this great nation" (1 Ki. 5:7).

Solomon spent seven years building God's temple (1 Ki. 6:38). There was a big dedication ceremony and prayer when the temple was finished, with all of Israel gathered together. Part of his prayer of dedication was this:

> As for the foreigner who does not belong to your people Israel but has come from a distant land because of your name— for they will hear of your great name and your mighty hand and your outstretched arm—when they come and pray toward this temple, then hear from heaven, your dwelling place. Do whatever the foreigner asks of you, *so that all the peoples of the earth may know your name and fear you*, as do your own people Israel, and may know that this house I have built bears your Name (1 Ki 8:41-43, emphasis added).

Solomon was essentially praying that God would use His temple to draw the nations to Himself and bless them with His salvific Presence. He was praying the Abrahamic Covenant over the temple! Then he said:

> And may these words of mine, which I have prayed before the Lord, be near to the Lord our God day and night, that he may uphold the cause of his servant and the cause of his people Israel according to each day's need, *so that all the peoples of the earth may know that the Lord is God and that there is no other* (1 Ki. 8:59-61, emphasis).

What an amazing prayer of dedication that highlights Solomon's understanding of the covenant. God heard his prayer and renewed the promise He had made with David to "establish [his] royal throne over Israel forever" (1 Ki. 9:5). The Lord also gave Solomon a stern warning. He said that if he or his descendants failed to keep the covenant, failed to observe God's decrees and commands, or turned to false idols, He would "cut off Israel from the land… and reject this temple [that was] consecrated for [His] name" (1 Ki. 9:6-7).

Chapter ten records a story where Solomon's prayer for the temple comes to fruition. The queen of Sheba came from afar because she had "heard about the fame of Solomon and his relationship to the Lord" (1 Ki. 10:1). After testing his wisdom, asking him hard questions, and seeing his great wealth as well as the way he worshiped the Lord, she was impressed and overwhelmed (1 Ki. 10:1-5). She then said to Solomon:

> The report I heard in my own country about your achievements and your wisdom is true. But I did not believe these things until I came and saw with my own eyes. Indeed, not even half was told me; in wisdom and wealth you have far exceeded the report I heard. How happy your people must be! How happy your officials, who continually stand before you and hear your wisdom! *Praise be to the Lord your God, who has delighted in you and placed you on the throne of Israel. Because of the Lord's eternal love for Israel, he has made you king to maintain justice and righteousness* (1 Ki. 10:6-9).

What a resounding endorsement! In fact, later in the chapter it says, "The whole world sought audience with Solomon to hear the wisdom God had put in his heart" (1 Ki. 10:24). Clearly God was blessing Solomon in order to bless the whole world. The nation of Israel was drawing the nations in for God's glory. This was a literal picture of Israel living out their purpose in being chosen in the center of the nations.

As J. Michael Thigpen says, "Solomon's reign is virtually synonymous with wisdom."[22] However, as time went on, he showed his propensity toward the things of this world. "As such, we see the wisest man become the greatest fool, as he led his family and nation into idolatry, division, and divine punishment."[23] As soon as the kingdom was established in his hands (1 Ki. 2:46), the very next paragraph in the narrative shows Solomon taking a foreign wife. In doing so, he created an alliance with Egypt. Furthermore, he did not just allow but also participated in sacrifices "on the high places" (1 Ki. 3:1-3). Woodhouse argues that marrying Pharoah's daughter was, "a sign that [Solomon's] kingdom had become a substantial empire, with a status at least equal to the great power of Egypt" and furthermore, an allusion to the

---

[22] J. Michael Thigpen, "Our Representational Reign: Royal Leadership in the United Monarchy," in *Biblical Leadership: Theology for the Everyday Leader*, ed. Benjamin Forrest and Chet Roden (Grand Rapids, MI: Kregel Academic, 2017), 133.

[23] Ibid., 133.

fulfillment of the Abrahamic Covenant, where all nations would be blessed through the nation of Israel. [24] Solomon, however, was not *leading* his foreign wives or their nations to Yahweh. Rather, they would eventually lead Solomon *away from* Yahweh. Solomon failed in obedience to every single one of the Deuteronomic commands for the king. Everything that God clearly stated a king of Israel must not do, Solomon did, and he did them in excess. He acquired "great numbers of horses" (Deut 17:16; 1 Ki 4:26, 10:26-28); he took "many wives" from nations whom the Lord forbid intermarriage and who led his heart astray (Deut 17:17; 1 Ki 11:1-5); and he accumulated "large amounts of silver and gold" (Deut 17:17; 1 Ki 9:14, 9:28, 10:2, 10:10, 10:14-27). All of these excesses were more from a heart of military security than a desire for worldly wealth. As mentioned earlier, the people wanted a king to lead them in battle because they did not trust in the Lord's provision and protection. Solomon's actions eventually affirmed that he felt the same way. Solomon's was a heart "not fully devoted to the Lord his God, as the heart of David his father had been" (1 Ki 11:4). In the end, all of the warnings and admonishments from the Deuteronomic law, from his father David, and directly from Yahweh Himself played out exactly as they had been presented to him.

In a fascinating article on the diplomatic and economic perspective of king Solomon's reign, Yosef Green explores the "political and economic acumen" of Solomon, and how "Israel's commerce, trade and industry during his reign" display "political and administrative wisdom."[25] Certainly this is true, and one could easily argue that this would contribute to the fulfillment of the Abrahamic Covenant. As industry and trade routes went through the Promised Land, the hope was that many more nations would come through and "the law [would] go out from Zion, the word of the Lord from Jerusalem" (Is. 2:3). Through prosperity, God would display His splendor through Israel (Is. 49:5) in order that "salvation may reach to the ends of the earth" (Is. 49:6). However, prosperity was not the primary means through which God intended to show the world His glory through Israel. They were to be set apart in holiness (Ex. 19:5-6). Disregarding the law of Moses would not display the glory of God to the nations, and that was where Solomon failed. His disobedient heart prevented blamelessness and holiness, and thus pushed away the presence of God.[26]

---

[24] John Woodhouse, *1 Kings: Power, Politics, and the Hope of the World* (Wheaton, IL: Crossway, 2018), 92-93.
[25] Yosef Green. "The Reign of King Solomon." *The Jewish Bible Quarterly.* 42, no. 3 (2014): 151.
[26] See 1 Thessalonians 3:13

In the end, wisdom does not equate to obedience. Solomon used his God-given wisdom in order to grow an empire. However, God had said to His people Israel, before they entered the land, that through obedience to His commands they would show "wisdom and understanding to the nations" (Deut. 4:6). Solomon eventually learned that wisdom in and of itself is meaningless (Ecc. 1:12-18). Not only that, but he also lamented throughout the book of Ecclesiastes that virtually everything was meaningless. Everything he had strived for and attained throughout his life due to his wisdom, all of it was meaningless to him. The only thing that truly mattered in the end was to "fear God and keep his commandments" (Ecc. 12:13). A life not spent glorifying God and working to see His name glorified among the nations is a life that amounts to nothing.

The reason we spent more time on Solomon than David is because the consequences of his lifestyle would have repercussions for generations to come. David was a man after God's own heart whose entire life was worshipful and obedient, with a few exceptions. Solomon, however, lived a life fully devoted to himself, with a few exceptions. Solomon's wives (i.e., political alliances) "led him astray. As [he] grew old, his wives turned his heart after other gods, and his heart was not fully devoted to the Lord his God, as the heart of David his father had been" (1 Ki. 11:3-4). Because of that, "the Lord became angry with Solomon because his heart had turned away from the Lord, the God of Israel, who had appeared to him twice" (1 Ki. 11:9). Imagine having encounters with God like Solomon did and still turning to idols and false gods. As a result, the Lord said:

> Since this is your attitude and you have not kept my covenant and my decrees, which I commanded you, I will most certainly tear the kingdom away from you and give it to one of your subordinates. Nevertheless, for the sake of David your father, I will not do it during your lifetime. I will tear it out of the hand of your son. Yet I will not tear the whole kingdom from him, but will give him one tribe for the sake of David my servant and for the sake of Jerusalem, which I have chosen (1 Ki. 11:11-13).

Solomon's disobedience and disregard for the covenant eventually led to a split in the nation of Israel from which they would never fully recover. The tribes were split into the northern kingdom, which remained as Israel, and the southern kingdom, which became known as Judah. As the author of Chronicles says, "So Israel has been in rebellion against the house of David to this day" (2 Chron. 10:19).

DIVIDED

The kingdom of Israel became divided in 931 B.C.. For 200 years, the northern kingdom had one bad king after another. They fought amongst themselves, worshiped idols and false gods, and abandoned the covenant with Yahweh. Then, in 722 B.C., Assyria conquered the northern kingdom of Israel. As for Judah, they stayed in the land a bit longer than Israel because they occasionally had a king who would turn the people's hearts back to the Lord. However, in 605 B.C., they suffered a similar fate as Israel when they were conquered by Babylon and taken into exile. The rest of the books of 1 & 2 Kings and 2 Chronicles tell the stories of this divided period of time and the downward spiral of God's chosen nation. God had warned them countless times that this would happen. The book of Deuteronomy is filled with admonitions to uphold the covenant or suffer this fate. God had told Solomon:

> **If you turn away and forsake the decrees and commands I have given you and go off and serve other gods and worship them, then I will uproot Israel from my land, which I have given them, and will reject this temple I have consecrated for my Name. I will make it a byword and an object of ridicule among all peoples. This temple will become a heap of rubble (2 Chron. 7:19-21).**

Thus became the fate of God's chosen people. They turned away from God and the covenant. Therefore, God uprooted them from the land, rejected the temple, and removed His presence from among them.

Thinking back on God's original plan for His chosen nation, we can see the severity of their idol worship. While they had the land, they were still the city on a hilltop that could not be hidden. They were still the center of the known world. They were still on center stage for all the world to see. God would not tolerate any confusion as to who was blessing this people. How were the nations supposed to hear of the great fame of the God of Israel with other gods in the way? God was supposed to be set apart so that they knew that He was the God of all gods and greatest in all the earth.

Throughout this time, God sent prophets in an attempt to convince His people to turn back to Him and His covenant with them. He had said to Solomon that even when He sent judgment and calamity on His people, "If my people, who are called by my name, will humble themselves and pray and seek my face and turn from their wicked ways, then I will hear from heaven, and I will forgive their sin and will heal their land" (2 Chron. 7:14). Sometimes in Judah they responded positively to the words of the prophets and repented. They would then experience a period of peace and testing, usually forty years. However, time and time again, they would slip right back into their idolatry and wickedness.

Despite their obstinate disobedience, God was still orchestrating His plan to draw the nations back to Himself. Even in the midst of, and at times in spite of, Israel's disobedience and willful apostasy, God continued to use them. One example is the story of Naaman, a Syrian military commander. He was "a great man in the sight of his master and highly regarded" (2 Ki. 5:1), but he was not an Israelite. In fact, he was often engaged in battle against Israel. In one of their military conflicts, Naaman's army had taken captives from among the Israelites. A young girl from Israel served as his wife's servant. When Naaman became afflicted with leprosy, the young girl told her mistress that there was a prophet in Israel that could heal him. Naaman went to the prophet Elisha for healing, and he did receive miraculous healing. He then said to Elisha, "Now I know that *there is no God in all the world except in Israel*" (2 Ki. 5:15, emphasis added). Naaman became a follower of the One True God because of his wife's Israelite slave girl. God was still drawing the nations to Himself, even in the midst of Israel's idolatrous distraction.

EXILE

The Lord had sent countless warnings but Israel "would not listen and were as stiff-necked as their ancestors, who did not trust in the Lord their God" (2 Ki. 17:14). They continued in their ways until their sin had reached its full measure.

> So the Lord was very angry with Israel and removed them from his presence. Only the tribe of Judah was left, and even Judah did not keep the commands of the Lord their God. They followed the practices Israel had introduced. Therefore the Lord rejected

> all the people of Israel; he afflicted them and gave them into the hands of plunderers, until he thrust them from his presence. When he tore Israel away from the house of David, they made Jeroboam son of Nebat their king. Jeroboam enticed Israel away from following the Lord and caused them to commit a great sin. The Israelites persisted in all the sins of Jeroboam and did not turn away from them until the Lord removed them from his presence, as he had warned through all his servants the prophets. So the people of Israel were taken from their homeland into exile in Assyria (2 Ki. 17:18-23).

The southern kingdom also went into exile.

> The Lord, the God of their ancestors, sent word to them through his messengers again and again, because he had pity on his people and on his dwelling place. But they mocked God's messengers, despised his words and scoffed at his prophets until the wrath of the Lord was aroused against his people and there was no remedy. He brought up against them the king of the Babylonians, who killed their young men with the sword in the sanctuary, and did not spare young men or young women, the elderly or the infirm. God gave them all into the hands of Nebuchadnezzar. They set fire to God's temple and broke down the wall of Jerusalem; they burned all the palaces and destroyed everything of value there. He carried into exile to Babylon the remnant, who escaped from the sword, and they became servants to him and his successors until the kingdom of Persia came to power (2 Chron. 36:15-17, 19-20).

For hundreds of years, God had warned His people that this would happen, and they did not believe Him. They mocked the prophets, relied on their own strength and understanding, and appealed to false gods and idols for protection. God would not make an idol of the temple built to house His Presence. As glorious as it was, His Presence could not and would not reside among the unholy. When His people became defiled by their own sin and disobedience, His Presence left the temple, and He sent Israel's enemies to destroy it brick by brick.

Yet, even in exile, God's purpose prevailed. The book of Daniel is set during the exilic period. Daniel was part of the remnant sent to Babylon when Jerusalem fell and the southern kingdom of Judah was conquered. There are two stories, both fairly familiar to most Christians and Jews, that highlight God's covenant with Abraham at work despite the exile. The first is in the story of Shadrach, Meshach, and Abednego, found in chapter three. These three friends got caught worshiping Yahweh, which was illegal in Babylon. They were brought in front of the king for judgment, and they said:

> King Nebuchadnezzar, we do not need to defend ourselves before you in this matter. If we are thrown into the blazing furnace, the God we serve is able to deliver us from it, and he will deliver us from Your Majesty's hand. But even if he does not, we want you to know, Your Majesty, that we will not serve your gods or worship the image of gold you have set up (Dan. 3:16-18).

Then they were thrown into the furnace and a mysterious fourth person was seen with them, one who looked like "a son of the gods" (Dan. 3:25). The three friends miraculously walked out of the fire unscathed, without so much as the smell of fire on their clothing (Dan. 3:27). The king was shocked. He said:

> Praise be to the God of Shadrach, Meshach and Abednego, who has sent his angel and rescued his servants! They trusted in him and defied the king's command and were willing to give up their lives rather than serve or worship any god except their own God. Therefore I decree that the people of any nation or language who say anything against the God of Shadrach, Meshach and Abednego be cut into pieces and their houses be turned into piles of rubble, *for no other god can save in this way* (Dan. 3:28-29, emphasis added).

King Nebuchadnezzar publicly praised Yahweh! The blessing of reconciliation and God's presence had come to Babylon. Even in exile and punishment, God was still using Israel as a display of His great name to the nations.

During that same period in exile, another king came to power and once again, God used His people to glorify His name among the Babylonians. In chapter six, Daniel was the one who got caught worshiping the God of Israel. This time the worship prohibition had come more as a trap for Daniel than a true conviction from the king. However, a decree was a decree, and the king could not go back on it (Dan. 6:12-14). Daniel was thrown into a den of hungry lions much to the dismay of a worried king Darius. "God sent his angel, and he shut the mouths of the lion" so Daniel was saved (Dan. 6:22). King Darius then revoked the old decree and issued a new one:

> King Darius wrote to all the nations and peoples of every language in all the earth: "May you prosper greatly! I issue a decree that in every part of my kingdom people must fear and reverence the God of Daniel. *For he is the living God and he endures forever,* his kingdom will not be destroyed, his dominion will never end. He rescues and he saves; he performs signs and wonders in the heavens and on the earth. He has rescued Daniel from the power of the lions (Dan. 6:25-27, emphasis added).

What a decree! God blessed Daniel in order to bless all the nations of the earth. Because of what seemed like the end of Daniel, all the nations heard from the king of Babylon that there is a God who saves.

Prophecy

PENDING JUDGMENT

God was working the entire time through Israel, but these were dark times indeed for God's people. The kingdom had been divided, the Israelites steadily declined into immorality, and eventually, as we have just seen, they were taken into exile. As has been mentioned, God sent countless warnings through His prophets, but the people did not listen. There are other themes seen throughout the prophets' messages that compel attention. Those will be the subjects of this next section. The intention is, again, not to create a commentary on the prophetic books of the Old Testament. The intention is to show the thread of the Abrahamic Covenant and the chosen nation's mission throughout Scripture.

Remember the golden calf and the test of an unfaithful wife incident at the base of Mount Sinai? God had chosen Israel in a way that was rich with marriage imagery. In the book of Hosea, God called the prophet Hosea to illustrate the unfaithfulness of Israel through an elaborate demonstration or object lesson. Hosea was to publicly marry a promiscuous woman and name their children for the pending judgment on Israel (Hos. 1:2-9). Hosea's prophecy dates right before the northern kingdom, Israel's, exile to Assyria. The entirety of the prophecy can be summarized by this verse: "When Israel was a child, I loved him, and out of Egypt I called my son. But the more they were called, the more they went away from me" (Hos. 11:1-2).

Hosea's object lesson marriage provided a powerfully accurate picture of Israel's disregard for her Bridegroom. Hosea's wife repeatedly left him to literally prostitute herself to other men. As shameful as this act is today, it was even more shameful back then. In fact, Hosea could have legally stoned his wife to death for her recurrent infidelity. But God called Hosea to keep allowing her to come back as an illustration of God's steadfast love, patience, and forgiveness of Israel. Although He said, "My God will reject them because they have not obeyed him; they will be wanderers among the nations" (Hos. 9:17), He also showed that their true repentance would never lead to rejection (Hos. 14). He would take them back over and over again if only they would return. His primary desire was "mercy, not sacrifice" (Hos. 6:6).

The prophet Amos came at a similar time and with a similar message. He brought oracles of judgment on six pagan nations plus the nations of Israel and Judah. An interesting thing to note is that the judgments being brought against the wicked foreign nations are not tremendously different than those brought against Israel/Judah. They all begin the same way, they indict similar offenses, and they end in God's judgment. In that way, we can see that Israel and Judah were being treated in the same way as the surrounding pagan nations despite their chosenness. There *should* have been noticeable differences between Israel/Judah and the surrounding nations. After all, they were set apart to be different from the other nations (Ex. 19:5-6). Robert Chisholm says that Israel/Judah "occupied a privileged position among the nations of the world … chosen as his special covenant people. He expected them to be a model society characterized by social justice."[27] The word from Amos highlights Israel's failure to uphold this standard. They truly did become like all the other nations. Instead of being set apart in holiness, they became influenced by their wicked neighbors. God said, "You only have I chosen of all the families of the earth; therefore I will punish you for all your sins" (Amos 3:2). In other words, to whom much privilege is given, much is expected.

The prophet Micah also warned of the impending judgment upon Israel (the northern kingdom, also called Samaria) and Judah. Chisholm notes:

> **These evildoers rejected the prophets who confronted them with their sinful actions. They wanted to hear promises of prosperity (symbolized by "wine and beer," see v. 2:11). They told the Lord's**

---

[27] Robert B. Chisholm, *Handbook on the Prophets* (Grand Rapids, MI: Baker Academic, 2009), 386.

prophets to stop their impassioned rhetoric of judgment, for they were confident that the Lord would not humiliate his people (2:6-7a). In response to their faulty reasoning, the Lord reminded them that he rewards only those who obey him (v.7b), not those who treat their countrymen like enemies and steal their property (vv. 8-9). Their sin would bring disaster on the land (v. 10).[28]

Then, Micah shifted his message from that of judgment to one of future hope. In chapter four, "Micah envisioned a time when the temple mount in Jerusalem would become the focal point of the world (4:1-3). The nations would stream to Jerusalem to learn the Lord's laws."[29] This was what the promised land was supposed to be all along! A place where God would teach Israel "his ways so that [they would] walk in his paths" with the intention being that "the law [would] go out from Zion, the word of the Lord from Jerusalem" (Mic. 4:2). Unfortunately, Israel had not done that and therefore, judgment was coming.

A PROPHESIED MESSIAH

As mentioned previously, prophecy often had immediate fulfillment, but it also had future fulfillment. The theme of the coming Messiah is clear to see for those who have eyes to see it. Of course, today we have the benefit of the New Testament to easily see and compare the prophecies of old with the coming of Jesus. Up until this point, we have tried to abide by the story of Israel without introducing too many themes or concepts from the New Testament. For the benefit of Jewish readers, I have wanted to tell their story from their history. That history does intersect with Jesus of Nazareth in the first century; however, I have intentionally set aside the introduction of that to its proper time chronologically in God's big story. In this section, I will footnote references to the New Testament where applicable, but the text will remain primarily focused on the Old Testament.

The next chapter in the book of Micah introduced a promised ruler who would come from Bethlehem. It says:

> But you, Bethlehem Ephrathah, though you are small among the

---

[28] Chisholm, *Handbook on the Prophets*, 420.
[29] Ibid., 421-422.

> clans of Judah, out of you will come for me one who will be ruler over Israel, whose origins are from of old, from ancient times. Therefore Israel will be abandoned until the time when she who is in labor bears a son, and the rest of his brothers return to join the Israelites. He will stand and shepherd his flock in the strength of the Lord, in the majesty of the name of the Lord his God. And they will live securely, for then his greatness will reach to the ends of the earth (Micah 5:2-4).[30]

This is rich with symbolism of a coming Messiah. Bethlehem was the hometown of David (1 Sam 16:1). He would be from ancient times[31] and He would gather His fellow Israelites to fulfill what Israel had not been able to do... reach the ends of the earth with the blessing of Abraham. The "rest of his brothers," the Gentiles, would then join the Israelites. All nations would be blessed with relational reconciliation with God.

This idea of a coming Messiah is a major theme throughout the prophets. God spoke to His prophets words of judgment and condemnation, but then said that a Deliverer and Redeemer would come. This Messiah would come to usher in a new way to complete the task that had been given to Israel. Zechariah said:

> "Shout and be glad, Daughter Zion. For I am coming, and I will live among you," declares the Lord. *"Many nations will be joined with the Lord in that day and will become my people. I will live among you and you will know that the Lord Almighty has sent me to you.* The Lord will inherit Judah as his portion in the holy land and will again choose Jerusalem. Be still before the Lord, all mankind, because he has roused himself from his holy dwelling" (Zech. 2:10-13, emphasis added).

The Lord Himself was coming to live among His people and when that day came, many nations would come to Him and be redeemed. God Himself would come and His Presence would once again reside among the people in order to fulfill His purpose.

In chapter three, Zechariah told a prophetic story about Joshua, or Jeshua, as the high priest wearing filthy clothes (Zech. 3:1-3). An angel came to remove the filthy

---

[30] Matthew 2:6
[31] John 17:5

clothes but when he did, he said, "See, I have taken away your *sin*" (Zech. 3:4, emphasis added).[32] The clothes were symbolic of the people's sins. This High Priest, Jeshua, would bear the sins of all people. He would "wear" their sin, their filthy clothes, but the Lord would then take it away from Jeshua and from the people. This High Priest would walk in obedience and then govern the Lord's house (Zech. 3:6-7). Through this Servant, who he calls "the Branch" (Zech. 3:8), God said, "I will remove the sin of this land in a single day" (v.9).[33] This Messiah would be for God's chosen people Israel, but not just for Israel.[34] Judah and Israel had been set apart to be a blessing to the nations but had not been able to fulfill that. God said that He would still use them to bless the nations because from them would come the Messiah who *would* fulfill that (Zech. 8:13). The Messiah would come to fulfill God's purpose, the purpose Israel had not been able to complete. Yet even in their failure, God *would* actually fulfill it through them because it would ultimately be done through the Messiah, who would come from this people.

Furthermore, Zechariah affirmed that the Messiah would come from Judah (Zech. 10:4). Judah would be the bow from which the Lord would launch His arrows (Zech. 9:13). Zechariah said, "Rejoice greatly, Daughter Zion! Shout, Daughter Jerusalem! See, your king comes to you, righteous and having salvation, lowly and riding on a donkey, on a colt, the foal of a donkey…He will proclaim peace to the nations. His rule will extend from sea to sea and from the [Euphrates] River to the ends of the earth" (Zech. 9:9-10).[35] That the Messiah would come from Judah upholds the promises God made to David and Solomon. He was coming to proclaim peace and blessing and reconciliation to the nations. His reign would start from the border of the promised land (the Euphrates, Gen. 15:18) and extend to all the ends of the earth.[36]

Another interesting note in Zechariah is verse 11:14 that says, "Then I broke my second staff called Union, breaking the family bond between Judah and Israel." When the Assyrians conquered the northern kingdom, aka Israel, in 722 B.C., the Israelites from those tribes were scattered and dispersed. Many have called them the

---

[32] Luke 1:29
[33] Hebrews 9:28; 1 Peter 2:24; 1 John 2:2, 3:5
[34] Matthew 10:6; 15:21-28
[35] Matthew 21:6-11
[36] Acts 1:8

Ten Lost Tribes of Israel. However, when the Babylonians conquered the southern kingdom, aka Judah, they kept the population of Judeans together, thus retaining their religion and identity. The Lord showed great favor to the tribe of Judah, keeping a "watchful eye over the house of Judah" (Zech. 12:4) and making them greater (Zech. 12:7-9). From Judah would come one who would be "pierced" and bring about mourning like that of one who lost a firstborn son (Zech. 12:10-14).[37] However, on that very day, "a fountain [would] be opened to the house of David and the inhabitants of Jerusalem, to cleanse them from sin and impurity" (Zech. 13:1).[38] The Messiah, from the tribe of Judah and the house of David, would cleanse the people finally and fully of their sin.

Joel spoke similarly of the coming Messiah, saying that when the Lord came to dwell among His people, "all the ravines of Judah will run with water. A fountain will flow out of the Lord's house" (Joel 3:18).[39] He also said that in the day of the Messiah's coming, "I will pour out my Spirit on all people. Your sons and daughters will prophesy; your old men will dream dreams, your young men will see visions. Even on my servants, both men and women, I will pour out my Spirit in those days…and everyone who calls on the name of the Lord will be saved" (Joel 2:28-29, 32).[40] The Messiah would usher in a new age, an age marked by the coming of God's Spirit not to a temple built by human hands but rather, to all people. God's Holy Spirit, His Presence, would be poured out on *all* people to accomplish God's purpose.

Thus far, we have looked mostly at the minor prophets. They are called as such not because their prophecies are less important or valid, but they typically were not what we would consider a career prophet. They may have received one message or just a few messages from the Lord for a specific occasion. The major prophets tended to have a longer period of time in which they were operating in the prophetic. They received many revelatory words from God and therefore, the books of the major prophets are much longer. The scope of this book will not allow for a deep dive into all prophecy. Rather, let us once again take a high-level view of some of these with the intention of gaining further understanding of God's chosen people and the mission they were chosen to complete.

---

[37] John 19:34
[38] John 7:38
[39] John 7:38
[40] Acts 2:21; Romans 10:13

JEREMIAH, THE WEEPING PROPHET

Jeremiah came after the fall of the northern kingdom and after the prophet Isaiah. He was a prophet to Jerusalem, the city for which he wept, for about forty years. Most of his prophetic message is that of judgment coming on Judah and Jerusalem. God said through Jeremiah that Israel was holy to Him (Jer. 2:3). He said, "How gladly would I treat you like my children and give you a pleasant land, the most beautiful inheritance of any nation. I thought you would call me 'Father'" (Jer. 3:19). Instead, Israel was like an unfaithful wife (Jer. 3:20), exchanging her "glorious God for worthless idols" (Jer. 2:11), forsaking Him and going her own way (v.13).

Even still, God would allow His unfaithful bride to return if only she put away the "detestable idols," no longer go astray, and return to the covenant of the Lord (Jer. 4:1-2). But she would not (reminiscent of Hosea's prophecy). God reminded them of the covenant they had made and showed them all the ways they broke it. Judgment would come through drought, famine, and the sword (Jer. 5:17). He said to them, "Your own conduct and actions have brought this on you. This is your punishment" (Jer. 4:18).

However, like the other prophets, Jeremiah also prophesied about the coming Messiah. In a scathing judgment against the shepherds of Israel (the priests and the kings), the Lord put the blame on them for scattering His flock (Jer. 23:1-2). But then He said He would gather the remnant Himself. "The days are coming," declares the Lord, "when I will raise up for David a righteous Branch, a King who will reign wisely and do what is just and right in the land. In his days Judah will be saved and Israel will live in safety. This is the name by which he will be called: The Lord Our Righteous Savior" (Jer. 23:3, 5-6). Then, Jeremiah repeated almost those exact words again ten chapters later:

> "The days are coming," declares the Lord, "when I will fulfill the good promise I made to the people of Israel and Judah. In those days and at that time I will make a righteous Branch sprout from David's line; he will do what is just and right in the land. In those days Judah will be saved and Jerusalem will live in safety. This is the name by which it will be called: The Lord Our Righteous Savior" (Jer. 33:14-16).

God said that at that time, He would make the descendants of David "and the Levites who minister before [Him] as countless as the stars in the sky and as measureless as the sand on the seashore" (Jer. 33:22). This statement is a prophetic fulfillment of both the Abrahamic Covenant and the choosing of the chosen people in Exodus 19 at Mount Sinai. The Levites were the priests. God is saying that the descendants of David/Abraham would become His "kingdom of priests" (Ex. 19:5-6).[41]

Lastly, for the sake of this topic, Jeremiah mentions a new covenant coming. The Lord said through Jeremiah:

> "The days are coming," declares the Lord, "when I will make a new covenant with the house of Israel and with the house of Judah. It will not be like the covenant I made with their ancestors when I took them by the hand to lead them out of Egypt, because they broke my covenant, though I was a husband to them," declares the Lord. "This is the covenant I will make with the people of Israel after that time," declares the Lord. "I will put my law in their minds and write it on their hearts. I will be their God, and they will be my people. No longer will they teach their neighbor, or say to one another, 'Know the Lord,' because they will all know me, from the least of them to the greatest," declares the Lord. "For I will forgive their wickedness and will remember their sins no more" (Jer. 31:31).[42]

In Deuteronomy, God had told the people to bind these words of His to their wrists and foreheads, to which many devout Orthodox Jews take literally, tying small boxes that hold scrolls of Scripture to their wrists and heads (Deut. 6:8). Under the new covenant, the law would not be an external set of rules to follow. Rather, it would be a law of conscience, written not on the hands and forehead, but on the hearts and minds of His followers. Ezekiel would describe it as God giving them "an undivided heart and a new spirit in them," removing their "heart of stone and [giving] them a heart of flesh" (Ez.11:19). God would give them "a new heart and put a new spirit in [them]," saying, "I will put my Spirit in you and move you to follow my decrees and be careful to keep my laws" (Ez. 36:26-27). The new covenant would live inside each one of them.[43]

---

[41] 1 Peter 2:9-10
[42] Hebrews 8, 10
[43] John 14:15-26; 16:13-15

EZEKIEL AND JONAH

Ezekiel prophesied around the same time as Jeremiah, right before Judah was conquered. Jonah had been on the scene hundreds of years prior in the northern kingdom of Israel. These two prophets lived in vastly different eras of time and were called to vastly different things, but a reason will be shown for including them together. Ezekiel was a career prophet like Jeremiah and Isaiah, called to bring the tribes of Israel and Judah back into repentance. Jonah was also a prophet like them. The difference was that Jonah's assignment, as recorded in the book that bears his name, was a very different assignment.

Much could be written about the book of Ezekiel and certainly much has. He, of course, called Judah to repentance for their idolatry and warned of pending judgment and exile. He used powerful demonstrations and object lessons to communicate his point, like making a bread of God's judgment and cooking it over a fire made of feces (Ez. 4). (I often wonder if the popular health food craze of Ezekiel's Bread would be as lauded over if more people read their Bibles. Hopefully that one is not cooked over flaming feces. But it is still the bread of God's judgment.) Ezekiel also used some very graphic sexual imagery to describe Israel's promiscuous and adulterous ways.

God does not mince words about how tragically profaned His name had become among the nations because of Israel and Judah. He said:

> I had concern for my holy name, which the people of Israel profaned among the nations where they had gone. "Therefore say to the Israelites, 'This is what the Sovereign Lord says: It is not for your sake, people of Israel, that I am going to do these things, but *for the sake of my holy name*, which you have profaned among the nations where you have gone. I will show the holiness of my great name, which has been profaned among the nations, the name you have profaned among them. *Then the nations will know that I am the Lord*, declares the Sovereign Lord, when I am proved holy through you before their eyes'" (Ez. 36:21-23, emphasis added).

He then said that He would bring the people of Israel back to their own land, making them one nation under one king (Ez. 37:15-28). This king would be the new David and would rule forever, establishing an everlasting covenant of peace and a "sanctuary among them forever" (Ez. 37:25-26). "Then the nations will know that I the Lord make Israel holy" (Ez. 37:28). God would come as their shepherd (Ez. 34:10), to search for His sheep and find them (v.11), judging "between one sheep and another, and between rams and goats" (v.17).[44] God said, "I will place over them one shepherd, my servant David, and he will tend them; he will tend them and be their shepherd" (Ez. 34:23).[45]

In all of this, God's purpose never changed. Through the choosing of the chosen nation all the way through the judgment and exile, His purpose remained the same. "I will show my greatness and my holiness, and I will make myself known *in the sight of many nations*. Then they will know that I am the Lord" (Ez. 38:23, emphasis added). This is where Ezekiel and Jonah have an overlap in calling. When God first called Ezekiel, He said:

> **You are not being sent to a people of obscure speech and strange language, but to the people of Israel— not to many peoples of obscure speech and strange language, whose words you cannot understand. Surely if I had sent you to them, they would have listened to you. But the people of Israel are not willing to listen to you because they are not willing to listen to me, for all the Israelites are hardened and obstinate (Ez. 3:5-7).**

The Lord was stating that the nations would have been much more receptive to the word of the Lord than His own people were. In other words, the task that had been given to Israel would not have been met with resistance or disdain by the nations. The assignment would not have been terribly hard. However, they became so self-absorbed in their own chosenness and idolatry that they rarely even tried! A perfect picture of this is the story of Jonah.

Jonah often gets relegated to the children's Bible. Adults have a hard time with Jonah because it seems childish and unrealistic. Is it allegory or historically accurate? It is not placed in the historical section of the Old Testament, but it is also not placed in the poetic/literature section either. Jonah is right in the middle of the prophets.

---

[44] Matthew 25:31-46
[45] John 10:1-21

Furthermore, according to 2 Kings 14:25, there is a historical record of him prophesying during the reign of king Jeroboam II. For the purpose of this writing, let us set aside questions of whether or not he was actually alive and cognizant in the literal belly of a whale or fish for three days. Certainly, we can discard images of him with a lantern and knapsack warming his hands over a fire in said belly.

Jonah was a prophet sent on a mission to Nineveh. They were very much not Israelites. In fact, they were the enemy of Israel. Nineveh was the capital of Assyria, and the Assyrians were a long-time enemy of God's people, particularly the northern kingdom. When Jonah was sent there, he refused to go. He did not want to go because he thought that he was better than them. This story is a supernationalist picture of Israel. Their purpose was to preach salvation to the nations but over time, their chosenness blinded them to their mission. They felt as though certain nations did not deserve reconciliation with God. They felt His mercy should have limits, not for them of course, but for the other nations. Like an obstinate, obtuse, spoiled child, they whined loudly "That's not fair" whenever God showed favoritism to anyone else. They knew they were the chosen nation, but often they confused God's purpose for them with God's preference of them. God did not call them simply to bless them because they were God's favorite nation. On the contrary, God chose them to be an instrument of blessing to the whole earth. They were special in that they were chosen for a very special purpose. Unfortunately, they often lost sight of their purpose and only focused on their chosenness.

After Jonah's literal, legendary, or allegorical object lesson in the deep, he reluctantly agreed to go to Nineveh and proclaim, "Salvation comes from the Lord" (Jonah 2:9). Much to Jonah's surprise, "the Ninevites believed God" (Jon. 3:5). They repented and prayed for God's salvation to come. "But to Jonah this seemed very wrong, and he became angry" (Jon. 4:1). He essentially said to God, "I knew this would happen! I knew that they would repent, and You would forgive them, which is why I did not want to go in the first place. They don't deserve Your mercy because I don't like them! This isn't fair." God's people did not fulfill their mission to the nations. Furthermore, they became more wicked than the Ninevites had been. Yet unlike the Ninevites, no prophet could bring Israel to repentance. Eventually God's judgment would come on Israel through none other than the Assyrians, those who had believed and repented when called.

ISAIAH

Some have called the book of Isaiah a microcosm of the entire Bible, noting that the sixty-six chapters correspond to the sixty-six books of the Bible. Although I do not entirely subscribe to that view, I do firmly believe that Isaiah is a microcosm of the story of God's people, from original covenant to new covenant. Isaiah's prophetic career spanned about forty years and covered the time period before and during Israel's exile, as well as leading up to Judah's exile.

Isaiah, like the other prophets, contains much in terms of warning against pending judgment. The book starts with the Lord declaring, "I have reared children and brought them up, but they have rebelled against me. The ox knows its master, the donkey its owner's manger, but Israel does not know, my people do not understand" (Is. 1:2-3). Israel did not understand their role as God's servant to the nations. They turned their backs on Him and His covenant with them. Because of that, the promised land, which was once a good land flowing with milk and honey, now lay "desolate ... burned with fire ... stripped by foreigners" (Is. 1:7). Their offerings were meaningless (Is. 1:13) because the hearts of His people were deeply afflicted (v.5). Judgment was surely coming, as was exile "for their lack of understanding" (Is. 5:13). They had rejected the law (Is. 5:24) and therefore His anger burned against His people (v.25).

Furthermore, they failed to do the very thing that God had created them to do, which was to reflect His glory to the nations. Israel was supposed to be a "banner for the distant nations," calling out for "those at the ends of the earth" (Is. 5:26). Their chosenness was for a purpose and it was this: "I, the Lord, have called you in righteousness; I will take hold of your hand. I will keep you and will make you to be a *covenant* for the people and *a light for the Gentiles,* to open eyes that are blind, to free captives from prison and to release from the dungeon those who sit in darkness" (Is. 42:6-7, emphasis added).[46] But they failed. "We have not brought salvation to the earth, and the people of the world have not been reborn" (Is. 26:18). The Israelites did not bring salvation and redemption to all peoples of the earth.

However, God began declaring that He was going to do a new thing. "I am the Lord; that is my name! I will not yield my glory to another or my praise to idols.

---

[46] Luke 4

See, the former things have taken place, and new things I declare; before they spring into being I announce them to you" (Is. 42:8-9). God was going to introduce a new covenant:

> "But you, Israel, my servant, Jacob, whom I have chosen, you descendants of Abraham my friend, I took you from the ends of the earth, from its farthest corners I called you. I said, 'You are my servant'; I have chosen you and have not rejected you. So do not fear, for I am with you; do not be dismayed, for I am your God. I will strengthen you and help you; I will uphold you with my righteous right hand...For I am the Lord your God who takes hold of your right hand and says to you, Do not fear; I will help you. Do not be afraid, you worm Jacob, little Israel, do not fear, for I myself will help you," declares the Lord, your Redeemer, the Holy One of Israel (Is. 41:8-10, 13-14).

God Himself was going to come as the Helper. He Himself would do what Israel had failed to do. Immanuel, meaning "God with us," was going to come from the house of David (Is. 7:13). He would even give them a sign: "The virgin will conceive and give birth to a son, and will call him Immanuel" (Is. 7:14).[47] He said, "Forget the former things; do not dwell on the past. See, I am doing a new thing! ... I am making a way in the wilderness" (Is. 43:18-19).[48] However, the One coming would not be another prophet sent to bring Israel and Judah back to the covenant. Of Him, God said, "It is too small a thing for you to be my servant to restore the tribes of Jacob and bring back those of Israel I have kept. I will also make you *a light for the Gentiles, that my salvation may reach to the ends of the earth*" (Is. 49:6, emphasis added). The Messiah would restore Israel/Judah *and* fulfill her mission of bringing God's glorious, redemptive blessing to the ends of the earth.

His purposes never changed. He said, "Turn to me and be saved, all you ends of the earth; for I am God, and there is no other. By myself I have sworn, my mouth has uttered in all integrity a word that will not be revoked: Before me every knee will bow; by me every tongue will swear" (Is. 45:22-23).[49] This is the fulfillment of the Abrahamic Covenant. "Then the whole human race will know that I, the Lord, am

---

[47] Matthew 1:23
[48] Matthew 3:1-3
[49] Romans 14:11

your Savior, your Redeemer, the Mighty One of Jacob" (Is. 49:26). Of course, God would not forget His chosen people Israel. He said, "I have made you, you are my servant; Israel, I will not forget you. I have swept away your offenses like a cloud, your sins like a morning mist. Return to me, for I have redeemed you" (Is. 44:21-22). God's merciful willingness to accept Israel's repentance remains unending. He will always welcome them back into covenantal relationship with Him if they return with a sincerely repentant heart.

The foreigners and the outcast would also be welcomed in His Presence, alongside the Israelites (Is. 56:3-8). The nations would come, carrying the lost sheep of Israel in their arms and on their hips (Is. 49:22). This meant that under the new covenant, the scattered Israelites would be brought back to God. In a great reversal of roles, the nations would eventually minister to Israel and do for Israel what Israel had not done for the nations. God's house would truly be called "a house of prayer for all nations" (Is. 56:7).[50] Strangers and foreigners would be "called priests of the Lord" and "ministers of our God" (Is. 61:4-6) reminiscent of Exodus 19:5-6. The new covenant carried the same purpose, but simply a different instrument of fulfillment. The instrument of blessing under the old covenant was Israel. The instrument of blessing under the new covenant would be the Messiah, who would come through Israel. Even though Israel had failed, God Himself would keep the covenant. Just like He had promised Abraham in Genesis fifteen, the cutting of the covenant. God Himself would do it, and He would do it through Israel, whether Israel kept the covenant or not.

This new covenant through the coming Messiah would be "everlasting" (Is. 61:8-9). He said, "And I, because of what they have planned and done, am about to come and *gather the people of all nations and languages*, and they will come and see my glory" (Is. 66:18, emphasis added). Much of the book of Isaiah is a collection of prophetic messages where God was essentially saying to Israel, "You messed up… but for my Name's sake I won't destroy you. You messed up! But I still love you and I will redeem you. You messed up! But My purposes haven't changed, and someone is coming who will ultimately fulfill what you were not able to." The Messiah would come, and His name would be "God with us." The government would rest on His shoulders (Is. 9:6), and He would be called "Wonderful Counselor, Mighty God, Everlasting Father, Prince of Peace. Of the increase of his government and

---

[50] Matthew 21:13; Luke 19:46; Mark 11:9

peace there will be no end. He will reign on David's throne and over his kingdom, establishing and upholding it with justice and righteousness from that time on and forever. The zeal of the Lord will accomplish this" (Is. 9:6-7). The Messiah would be the fulfillment of the old covenant through the initiation of the new covenant, both of which had the purpose of reconciling all nations to God.

GREAT DISTRESS

Just as Jeremiah had said would happen, Babylon conquered and decimated Jerusalem and took God's people into exile for seventy years (Jer. 25). Eventually they were allowed to go back to their land, but not as an independent nation. They would be governed by the Persian Empire, arguably only allowed to return to their land and culture because of king Darius. Remember how he had had a powerful encounter with Yahweh through Daniel and the lions (Dan. 6)? He then allowed some of the exiles to return to Jerusalem and begin rebuilding (Ezra 6). Zerubbabel, governor of Judah, oversaw the rebuilding of the temple as prophesied by Haggai. Nehemiah, the layperson, oversaw the rebuilding of the walls surrounding Jerusalem. Ezra, the priest, would eventually bring the law back to God's people. Jerusalem was a far cry from what it had been in the days of David and Solomon, but God's people eventually got back to their land and began revitalizing the devastated city. They said, "For many years you were patient with [your people]. By your Spirit you warned them through your prophets. Yet they paid no attention, so you gave them into the hands of the neighboring peoples. But in your great mercy you did not put an end to them or abandon them, for you are a gracious and merciful God" (Neh. 9:30-31). It is impossible to study the history of God's people and come to any conclusion other than that God is *the* most merciful.

Abraham, Isaac, and Jacob lived in Canaan as foreigners. God brought His chosen people in and gave them the land as an inheritance and as owners (Deut. 1:8). However, their disobedience cost them the full blessing and favor of the Lord. Now only a remnant of God's people lived in the land, and this time not as foreigners or owners but as slaves (Neh. 9:36). They said, "But see, we are slaves today, slaves in the land you gave our ancestors so they could eat its fruit and the other good things it produces. Because of our sins, its abundant harvest goes to the kings you have placed over us. They rule over our bodies and our cattle as they please. We are in great distress" (Neh. 9:36-37). This was not God's original plan for His people in that land, though none of it surprised Him. Their free will choices had brought them to a devastating state of being. Apart from God's great mercy and His commitment to keep His covenant, who knows if He would have even spared this people.

For 400 years, there were no prophets bringing words from the Lord. The period between the Old and New Testaments, called the intertestamental period, was marked with silence. The people had a temple, but no Glory of God. They did not have the ark, or the tabernacle, and the Glory of God did not return to the second temple in the way that it had with the first temple. At least, not yet. They were a province governed by the Persian Empire until it was conquered by the Greek Empire (331 B.C.). Around this time, the land became known as Palestine. The Syrians also controlled Palestine for a period of time, as did the Seleucid Empire (280 B.C.). In 164 B.C., a family of devout followers of Yahweh led a revolt against the paganizing Seleucids in Palestine. "The temple mount was cleansed and rededicated...three years after it had been desecrated" by the ruler of the Seleucid Empire.[51] That family, the Hasmoneans, ruled Palestine until 63 B.C. when Rome conquered Jerusalem. As we can see, this land has seen a tremendous amount of bloodshed, war, and changing of hands not only in modern times, but truly going back nearly 4,000 years.

---

[51] Walter A. Elwell and Robert W. Yarbrough, *Encountering the New Testament: A Historical and Theological Survey*, 3rd ed. (Grand Rapids, MI: Baker Academic, 2013), 27.

Introduction to the New Testament

This is the part in history where Jewish and Christian beliefs typically diverge; however, if I have been honored enough to keep a Jewish reader this far into the story, I implore you to continue. A proper understanding of Christianity is not a replacement of Israel, but rather an extension and fulfillment of it. That topic will be explored in greater detail, but for now, a summary of previous sections will greatly assist in stepping into this next section.

God made a covenant with one man, Abraham, saying that through him and his descendants all nations would be blessed (Gen. 12:2-3). Those descendants became the chosen nation of Israel. Unfortunately, idolatry and rebellion pulled them further and further away from God and His covenant with them. Judgment and punishment came, but through the prophets God promised a Messiah who would ultimately fulfill the old covenant by initiating a new covenant. The purpose was the same, only the means to accomplish it would be different. The Messiah, however, would not look at all like what the people were expecting. After centuries of occupation in their land by powerful pagan empires, they expected a great warrior king like David to restore the land and the people to their former glory. After all, God had said the Messiah would come from the line of David and the branch of Jesse (Jesse was David's father). They envisioned an earthly throne where David and Solomon's descendant would reign forever. God had made that promise and yet Israel had not had a king since before the exile.

For those new to or unfamiliar with the New Testament, it starts with four books called the gospels. These are four different accounts of Jesus' time on earth. Four different people, three of whom are directly linked to those who followed Jesus and one who conducted interviews of eyewitnesses, all telling their version of the story.[52] They are written with different audiences in mind and are truly unique accounts of the same story. Three out of the four gospel accounts were written within forty years of the events they describe.[53] All four were written within the lifetime of eyewitnesses of those events. Even though there are minor discrepancies in some details of stories, the ways that they are told, and which stories are included in which gospel account, there is no discrepancy or disagreement among the four that disrupts anything foundational to the Christian faith. In the same way that four different people witnessing any event would describe it very differently based on their perspective, the gospels clearly tell the same story.

After the gospels is the books of Acts, also known as the Acts of the Apostles. This shows the expansion of the early Church after Jesus' time on earth. The rest of the New Testament, with the exception of Revelation, is a collection of historical letters written by the apostles to people and congregations in the early Church. Finally, Revelation is a prophetic vision from the apostle John.

---

[52] Elwell and Yarbrough, *Encountering the New Testament*, 59
[53] Ibid., 58

The Messiah

THE COMING OF THE MESSIAH

John's gospel begins by placing Jesus in the beginning of time and creation with God. It says:

> In the beginning was the Word, and the Word was with God, and the Word was God. He was with God in the beginning. Through him all things were made; without him nothing was made that has been made. In him was life, and that life was the light of all people. The light shines in the darkness, and the darkness has not overcome it ... The true light that gives light to everyone was coming into the world ... The Word became flesh and made his dwelling among us. We have seen his glory, the glory of the one and only Son, who came from the Father, full of grace and truth (John 1:1-5, 9, 14).

Jesus has been called the Incarnate Word of God. God's very Word, which was spoken in the beginning of time to bring forth life through His Spirit, eventually became flesh and dwelt among His creation. Imagine that for a minute. When God created the world, the Word that He spoke, saying "Let there be light," would become flesh and blood. That Word later took the form of a human man and dwelt among His own creation. God with us. Immanuel.

Jesus did not come the natural way because He was supernatural. Remember in the Garden of Eden, God said that the Redeemer would be born of woman. There is only one man, one person in history that was born *only* of woman. An angel appeared to an Israelite woman named Mary and said, "You have found favor with God. You will conceive and give birth to a son, and you are to call him Jesus. He will be great and will be called the son of the Most High. The Lord will give him the throne of his father David, and he will reign over the house of Jacob forever; His Kingdom will never end" (Luke 1:30-33). Mary asked how this was possible because she was a virgin and the angel replied, "The Holy Spirit will come on you, and the power of the Most High will overshadow you. So the holy one to be born will be called the Son of God" (Luke 1:35). Born of woman (Gen. 3:15), the virgin conceived and gave birth to a Son who would be Immanuel, God with us (Is. 7:14). "For to us a child is born, to us a son is given, and the government will be on his shoulders" (Is. 9:6). The one that the prophets spoke about was finally coming.

Mary was pledged to be married to a man named Joseph and, although he had every legal right to break their engagement when she was found to be pregnant, he was also visited by an angel of the Lord who corroborated Mary's unbelievable story. The angel said to Joseph, "Do not be afraid to take Mary home as your wife, because what is conceived in her is from the Holy Spirit. She will give birth to a son, and you are to give him the name Jesus, because he will save his people from their sins" (Matt. 1:20-21). Joseph became Jesus' father not through blood but through adoption, through his choosing. Matthew's gospel begins with a genealogy that traces Joseph's ancestral line from him, through Solomon and David, all the way back through Judah, Jacob, Isaac, and eventually Abraham (Matt. 1:1-16).

Women were not typically included in genealogies but in Matthew's gospel, we see five women listed, one of whom is Jesus' mother, Mary. The mother of Judah's sons, Tamar, is chronologically first. Although Scripture is not very clear on this, it is likely that Tamar was a Canaanite or of some other non-Israelite descent. The story of how she ended up in the genealogy is actually quite scandalous (Gen. 38). The second woman listed is Rahab, who has already been discussed. She was certainly not an Israelite and quite possibly a prostitute (Josh. 2). The third woman listed is Ruth. Ruth was a Moabite from the incestuous line of Lot (Gen. 19:30-38; Ruth 1). The Moabites and their descendants were not permitted to enter the assembly of the Lord (Deut. 23:3). Yet, she became the great-grandmother of king David

(Ruth 4:17-22) and thus honored in inclusion in the genealogy of Jesus. The fourth woman is Bathsheba, the woman David committed adultery with, which he then attempted to conceal by murdering her husband (2 Sam. 11). Her husband was a Hittite, which makes him a Gentile, and therefore it is likely that she was as well. What an interesting collection of women to add to the genealogy of the Messiah. This highlights the convergence of Jewish and Gentile blood into the new covenant. The Messiah had to be an Israelite, but this genealogy shows Him as a representative of Gentiles included in the family of God.

Luke also included a genealogy in his gospel, but his looks slightly different. It starts with Joseph as the son of Heli. Heli is believed to be the father of Mary, so Joseph's father-in-law. Therefore, Luke's genealogy is actually tracing Mary's family line, not Joseph's. This genealogy also puts Jesus in the family line of David and of Abraham. The reason this is important is because some would argue that Jesus was not of the bloodline of Joseph, since Joseph did not physically father him; however, the father's bloodline was important. Technically, Jesus had the most perfect bloodline from His Father. But the importance of fulfilling prophecy is shown in the fact that either way you slice it, Jesus came from the prophetically proclaimed Messianic bloodline.

Jesus was born in Bethlehem, not because it was His hometown, but because of a census that had been ordered by the Romans (Luke 2:1-4). This fulfilled the prophecy of Micah 5:2-4. The announcement of the birth of the Messiah came not first to the priests or to the royal leaders of the day but rather to a group of shepherds watching their flock at night (Luke 2:8-11). It is an interesting picture when viewed in light of Ezekiel's prophecy about the Lord coming as Israel's shepherd (Ez. 34). A host of angels appeared to those shepherds in Bethlehem that night and proclaimed that they brought "good news of great joy that will be for *all the people*" (Luke 2:10, emphasis added), a picture of what Isaiah had prophesied when he said, "How beautiful on the mountains are the feet of those who bring good news, who proclaim peace, who bring good tidings, who proclaim salvation, who say to Zion, 'Your God reigns!'" (Is. 52:7). In the town of David, the Messiah had been born (Luke 2:11).

In what would be today's equivalent of a baby dedication, the young Jesus was brought to the temple "for purification rites required by the Law of Moses" (Luke 2:22). There was a man named Simeon who was "righteous and devout" and who had the Holy Spirit on him (Luke 2:5). "It had been revealed to him by the

Holy Spirit that he would not die before he had seen the Lord's Messiah" (Luke 2:26). When he met the young Jesus, he proclaimed, "Sovereign Lord, as you have promised, you may now dismiss your servant in peace. For my eyes have seen your salvation, which you have prepared in the sight of all nations: a light for revelation to the Gentiles, and the glory of your people Israel" (Luke 2:29-32). A light for the Gentiles, but also the glory of Israel. He was Israel's fulfillment of the covenant. Now reconciliation would finally come to the Gentiles. He had come, as Isaiah had said, "to be a covenant for the people and a light for the Gentiles" (Is. 42:6).

Some of Jesus' first worshipers were "Magi from the east" (Matt. 2:1). The Magi were most assuredly Gentiles. The Israelites had been warned against gazing up at the stars for guidance, like the pagan nations did (Is. 47:13). Yet, God announced the arrival of the Messiah to even them ahead of His people Israel.

King Herod heard from the Magi of the east that the anticipated Messiah had been born (Matt. 2:1-8). In an attempt to squelch the possibility of a new king, Herod gave orders to kill all baby boys in Bethlehem ages two and under (Matt. 2:16). The Lord, however, had warned Joseph in a dream to take Mary and Jesus in the night and escape to Egypt (Matt. 2:12-15). When it was safe to return home, God once again called His Son out of Egypt (Matt. 2:14-15; Ex. 4:22-23; Hosea 11:1) and they returned to their hometown of Nazareth, fulfilling prophecies about the Messiah being a Nazarene (Matt. 2:23). So many details, all pointing to Jesus as the prophesied Messiah.

THE MINISTRY OF JESUS

Jesus' earthly ministry did not begin until He was thirty years old, and it only lasted three years. Not much is said in Scripture about His childhood, but we know that He was raised by a carpenter in the very unimpressive town of Nazareth. How could a carpenter's son from a redneck town in Roman-occupied Palestine, one of the least of all the Roman provinces, do anything of great significance in just three years? He never held political office or served in any military. He was not a religious leader of the time, though that would not have mattered much because the Romans mocked and despised the Jews and their odd beliefs. In His three years of ministry, He never even traveled more than a hundred miles from His own hometown, probably even less than that. His followers were hunted down, persecuted, and many were killed for the first three hundred years after His short ministry time. How on earth did His story ever make it out of the first century? I would contend that the stories contained in the four gospel accounts must be true. Otherwise, nobody on earth would have ever known about a carpenter's son from Nazareth.

There are five themes that I want to focus on throughout the gospels' portrayal of Jesus' earthly ministry. First, His interactions with His own people, the Israelites. Second, His intentionality in reaching out to those deemed unworthy by the religious elite of His day. Third, His radical teaching on the kingdom of God. Fourth, the authority and mission He gave to the Church. Finally, what His death and resurrection accomplished for all people and all nations (and it is so much more than where we spend eternity).

ONE: JESUS THE ISRAELITE

Jesus stepped into the first century as a fully devout Israelite. From the purification rituals and presentation at the temple (Luke 2:22-40) to the yearly pilgrimage to the temple in Jerusalem for the Festival of the Passover (vv.41-52), Scripture is clear that He was born into a devout Jewish family. He said in one of His most famous sermons, the Sermon on the Mount, "Do not think that I have come to abolish the Law or the Prophets: I have not come to abolish them but to fulfill them" (Matt. 5:17). A common misconception still today is that Jesus came to end the law of Moses. I think that misconception stems from the misunderstanding of the purpose of the law. As we already discussed, the law was a gift from God to Israel. It contained all the instructions they needed to live a life of holiness. The law helped restore the relationships between God and man, between man and woman, and between man and creation that were broken way back in the garden. It was about how to love God and love our neighbor, which Jesus said were the greatest commandments (Matt. 22:34-40). In fact, He said that "*all* the Law and the Prophets hang on these two commandments" (Matt. 22:40, emphasis added). Jesus was saying that in Him, the commands to love God and neighbor would be fulfilled.

Jesus spoke particularly harshly to the religious leaders when they held up the law not as an act of love, but as a tool used to control the people. Their traditional upholding of the law often placed keeping the rules above the relationships that the law was created to cultivate. Some of the religious leaders asked Jesus why His followers broke "the tradition of the elders" (Matt. 15:2). Jesus' response was, "Why do you break the command of God for the sake of your tradition?" (Matt. 15:3) If all the Law and the Prophets hang on the commands to love God and your neighbor, how can any law prohibit that? Jesus said, "You nullify the word of God for the sake of your tradition" (Matt. 15:6). Even this fulfilled prophecy, when Isaiah wrote, "These people honor me with their lips, but their hearts are far from me. They worship me in vain; their teachings are merely human rules" (Is. 29:13; Matt. 15:7-9). Jesus was a purer Israelite than any Israelite ever had been.

He also intentionally showed the ways that He was the fulfillment of the prophecies of old. Matthew's gospel in particular highlights this. Matthew was written for a Jewish audience and has more Old Testament references than the other three gospel accounts. When Jesus began His preaching ministry, Matthew shared that Jesus left His hometown of Nazareth and lived in Capernaum for a time (Matt. 4:13). Even this fulfilled prophecy from Isaiah when he said, "Land of Zebulun and land of Naphtali, the Way of the Sea, beyond the Jordan, Galilee of the Gentiles – the people living in darkness have seen a great light; on those living in the land of the shadow of death a light has dawned" (Matt. 4:14-16; Is. 9:1-2). The "Way of the Sea" was a major highway from Egypt to Damascus that passed right by the Sea of Galilee.

There were many specific prophecies, like that one, that He fulfilled. There were also parts of His ministry that fulfilled other Messianic prophecies. Matthew pointed out that His healing ministry fulfilled prophecy when Isaiah said, "He took up our infirmities and bore our diseases" (Matt. 8:17; Is. 53:4). All of the gospels mention John the Baptist, Jesus' cousin who came as a forerunner, announcing the arrival of Jesus. Luke intentionally showed where John fit into history, showing the exact year by highlighting which Roman officials were serving and who was the high-priest (Luke 3:1-2). All the gospels showed that John's ministry was the fulfillment of Isaiah's prophecy (Matt. 3:1-12; Mark 1:1-8; Luke 3:1-20; John 1:19-28; Is. 40:3). Matthew also showed how this fulfilled another prophecy from Malachi, that a messenger would first prepare the way for Him (Matt. 11:1-15; Mal. 3:1). Luke's account of John the Baptist uniquely concluded with the verse, "And all mankind will see God's salvation" (Luke 3:6; Is. 40:5).

Matthew also highlighted in fulfillment of prophecy that Jesus was the one in whom "the nations will put their hope" (Matt.12:21; Is. 42:4). The prophets had also stated that the Messiah's message would be a mystery to many, perhaps especially Israel. When Israel turned away from God toward the false gods surrounding them, they forgot their mission and purpose in being chosen. Jesus came to fulfill what they had forgotten. It is understandable why they would be "ever hearing but never understanding ... ever seeing but never perceiving. For this people's heart has become calloused; they hardly hear with their ears, and they have closed their eyes" (Matt. 13:14; Is. 6:9,10). Israel had long since forgotten their purpose and therefore, were unable to recognize the fulfillment of it, even when it was before their very eyes. He taught in parables and uttered "things hidden since the creation of the world" (Matt. 13:35; Ps 78:2).

Jesus' entire trial and death sentence fulfilled prophecy. Crucifixion was the Romans' brutal, torturous invention. It was found to be one of the most painful deaths possible. In fact, the term "excruciating" is derived from the word and concept of crucifixion. It had only been used by the Romans, so it was a relatively new concept; however, king David penned a psalm hundreds of years prior to the invention of crucifixion that seems to describe the circumstances of Jesus' death precisely.

My God, my God, why have you forsaken me? Why are you so far from saving me, so far from my cries of anguish? My God, I cry out by day, but you do not answer, by night, but I find no rest. (Ps. 22:1-2)

> About three in the afternoon Jesus cried out in a loud voice, "My God, my God, why have you forsaken me?" (Matt. 27:46, Mark 15:34)

Yet you are enthroned as the Holy One; you are the one Israel praises. In you our ancestors put their trust; they trusted and you delivered them. To you they cried out and were saved; in you they trusted and were not put to shame. But I am a worm and not a man, scorned by everyone, despised by the people. All who see me mock me; they hurl insults, shaking their heads. (Ps. 22:3-7)

> "Those who passed by hurled insults at him, shaking their heads and saying, "You who are going to destroy the temple and build it in three days, save yourself!"" (Matt. 27:39, Mark 15:29)

"He trusts in the Lord," they say, "let the Lord rescue him. Let him deliver him, since he delights in him." (Ps. 22:8)

> "The chief priests, teachers of the law, and elders said "He trusts in God. Let God rescue him now if he wants him, for he said, 'I am the Son of God.'" (Matt. 27:43)

I am poured out like water, and all my bones are out of joint. (Ps. 22:14a)

> "One of the soldiers pierced Jesus' side with a spear, bringing a sudden flow of blood and water." (John 19:34)

My heart has turned to wax; it has melted within me. My mouth is dried up like a potsherd, and my tongue sticks to the roof of my mouth. (Ps. 22:14b-15a)

> "Jesus said, "I am thirsty." A jar of wine vinegar was there, so they soaked a sponge in it, put the sponge on a stalk of the hyssop plant, and lifted it to Jesus' lips." (John 19:28)

You lay me in the dust of death. (Ps. 22:15b)

> "Joseph took [Jesus'] body, wrapped it in a clean linen cloth, and placed it in his own new tomb that he had cut out of a rock." (Matt. 27:60, Mark 15:46, Luke 23:53-54, John 19:39-42)

Dogs surround me, a pack of villains encircles me; (Ps. 22:16a)

> "Then the governor's soldiers took Jesus into the Praetorium and gathered the whole company of soldiers around him." (Matt. 27:27)

They pierce my hands and my feet. (Ps. 22:16b)

> "Then they led him out to crucify him." (Matt. 27:31, Mark 15:20, Luke 23:33, John 19:18)

The Messiah

All my bones are on display; people stare and gloat over me. (Ps. 22:17)

> "The people stood watching, and the rulers even sneered at him." (Luke 23:35, Mark 15:29-32)

They divide my clothes among them and cast lots for my garment. (Ps. 22:18)

> "When they had crucified him, they divided up his clothes by casting lots." (Matt. 27:35, Mark 15:24, Luke 23:34, John 19:24)

But you, Lord, do not be far from me. You are my strength; come quickly to help me. I will declare your name to my people; in the assembly I will praise you. You who fear the Lord, praise him! All you descendants of Jacob, honor him! Revere him, all you descendants of Israel! For he has not despised or scorned the suffering of the afflicted one; he has not hidden his face from him but has listened to his cry for help. The poor will eat and be satisfied; those who seek the Lord will praise him— may your hearts live forever! (Ps. 22:19, 22-24, 26)

> "Father, the hour has come. Glorify your Son, that your Son may glorify you. For you granted him authority over all people that he might give eternal life to all those you have given him. Now this is eternal life: that they know you, the only true God, and Jesus Christ, whom you have sent. I have brought you glory on earth by finishing the work you gave me to do. And now, Father, glorify me in your presence with the glory I had with you before the world began." (John 17:1-5)

All the ends of the earth will remember and turn to the Lord, and all the families of the nations will bow down before him, for dominion belongs to the Lord and he rules over the nations. They will proclaim his righteousness, declaring to a people yet unborn: He has done it! (Ps. 22:27-28, 31)

> "Then Jesus came to them and said, "All authority in heaven and on earth has been given to me. Therefore go and make disciples of all nations, baptizing them in the name of the Father and the Son and the Holy Spirit, and teaching them to obey everything I

have commanded you. And surely I am with you always, to the very end of the age.'" (Matt. 28:18-19)

JESUS THE ISRAELITE CALLS HIS OWN

Jesus hand-selected twelve apostles from among His followers "that they might be with him and that he might send them out to preach" (Mark 3:14). He endowed them with His authority to heal the sick and cast out demons. The gospels all share stories of how He chose the twelve that He chose, but none of them were particularly impressive for the task. He chose some fishermen right off of their boats (Matt. 4:18-22) and a religious zealot, who would have been viewed as an extremist from all sides. He also chose a tax-collector, who was the most offensive of all Jews because he was seen as a traitor of Israel, getting rich off the backs of his own people by enforcing Roman tax collection (Matt. 9:9-13). They would doubt Him, question Him, almost all nearly abandon Him in His time of greatest need, and one would even betray Him to His enemies. They were nothing at all like the religious elite of the time and that seems to be precisely why they were chosen.

When He first sent them out, He gave an interesting commission that often goes unnoticed. He said, "Do not go among the Gentiles or enter any town of the Samaritans. Go rather to the lost sheep of Israel. As you go, proclaim this message: 'The kingdom of heaven has come near.' Heal the sick, raise the dead, cleanse those who have leprosy, drive out demons" (Matt. 10:5-8). How do we reconcile this with what we know of His mission and what we know about the prophecies about Him? There is also a story where He had a weird interaction with a Canaanite woman that seems to undermine His Gentile mission. This woman came to Jesus asking Him to heal her daughter and His response was, "I was only sent to the lost sheep of Israel" (Matt. 15:24). Jesus did come for the entire world, Jews and Gentiles. However, there was an order of the way things should happen.

The twelve Jewish disciples are a picture of the twelve tribes of Israel. Through the twelve, He set out to accomplish what the twelve tribes had not been able to. God, in His endless mercy, was giving His chosen people yet another chance to do what they were chosen to do. He was blessing them once again with an opportunity to partake in the covenant and be a blessing to the nations. He did this when He healed the Jewish man of leprosy but told him not to tell anyone. He needed only to get right with God again (Matt. 8:4). Also, when he raised a synagogue leader's daughter from the dead (Matt. 9:18-26). He also told the Jewish men healed of blindness not to tell anyone (Matt. 9:27-30). His early ministry was focused on bringing as many Israelites as possible back into the covenant first in order that they might walk in their calling. Even though Jesus came as a fulfillment of the old covenant, God was not finished with His chosen people. He wanted them to fully participate in the new covenant as well.

In the interaction with the Canaanite woman, Jesus did end up healing her daughter. He said that He had only been sent to the lost sheep of Israel, but she persisted in her faithful imploring. In what comes across as uncharacteristically insensitive, He said, "It is not right to take the children's bread and toss it to the dogs" (Matt. 15:26). Did He really call that woman a dog? In our modern culture, that has a much different connotation than it would have had back then. Let's consider another perspective here. Obviously, we do not have the luxury of hearing His tone of voice when He spoke this. When she first asked, Jesus did not even respond. Perhaps He was testing His disciples. If so, their response was quite telling. They said, "Send her away, for she keeps crying out after us" (Matt. 15:23). At this point, everyone knew the disciples' heart posture toward this woman. Mark records Jesus' response as "First let the children eat all they want, for it is not right to take the children's bread and toss it to the dogs" (Mark 7:27). Everyone would have known what He meant by this. Israel was God's firstborn son, after all. The Canaanites were Israel's historic enemy, the ones who led the Israelites into idolatry after the Israelites failed to rid the land of them.

In faith she said, "Even the dogs eat the crumbs that fall from their master's table" (Matt. 15:27). In saying this, she was first implying that she recognized Israel as God's chosen son. Second, she recognized the God of Israel as the Master of all, the children and the dogs. Lastly, she was stating that even crumbs and leftovers from the Master's table are enough to sustain and give life. Despite her Canaanite roots, her humble faith was commended as "great faith" by Jesus, and her daughter was healed (Matt. 15:28). I would also contend that the disciples may have learned a powerful lesson here. Like Jonah, their unwillingness to respond to the needs of a Gentile and perceived enemy was met with Jesus' compassion and the Gentile's repentance.

TWO: JESUS FOR ALL

The Israelites of Jesus' day were expecting a Messiah who would restore them and their kingdom to its former glory, like the days of king David and king Solomon. Israel had been controlled by occupying forces for almost 700 years, from the time of Judah's exile to Babylon all the way to the Roman occupation of the first century. Jesus did not look anything like what they expected. After He chose the twelve and then sent them out to the lost sheep of Israel (Matt. 10:5-8), He broadened His ministry. He "appointed seventy-two others and sent them two by two ahead of him to every town and place where he was about to go. He told them, 'The harvest is plentiful, but the workers are few. Ask the Lord of the harvest, therefore, to send out workers into his harvest field'" (Luke 10:1-2). The twelve disciples were a picture of the twelve tribes. The seventy-two sent ones highlight another important picture. Going all the way back to Genesis chapter ten, we saw the table of nations created as a result of the tower of Babel. That chapter lists seventy-two nations. Howell says, "The symbolism seems to be that Jesus was sending out missionaries of the kingdom that correspond to the number of (ethnic) nations on earth and thus a harbinger of the coming universal proclamation of the gospel."[54] Jesus was relaunching the mission of the chosen people, first through His twelve chosen disciples, then multiplying it out from them to the nations.

The actions of Jesus' earthly ministry showed God's heart for His chosen people Israel, as well as the rest of the world. "From Adam onward, there is one human race and one flow of time, with all nations, Jews and gentiles, and all people, men and women, seen as universally loved by God and prospective recipients of salvation."[55] Collectively, the gospels all show that God sent His Son Jesus as the Savior of the whole world and the Redeemer of all people.

As mentioned previously, Matthew's gospel spoke more specifically to a Jewish audience. Luke's specifically emphasized and highlighted stories of salvation coming to those whom society at the time deemed outsiders, unworthy, and of lesser value. One "distinctive characteristic of Luke is its emphasis on the universal or comprehensive nature of God's dealings with the world."[56] Unlike Matthew's genealogy, which traced the lineage of Jesus back to Abraham, Luke carried the lineage all the

---

[54] Howell, *Servants of the Servant*, 147.
[55] Elwell and Yarbrough, *Encountering the New Testament*, 91.
[56] Ibid., 87.

way back to Adam. Matthew traced the lineage of Jesus back to Abraham, the father of *many* nations, whereas Luke traced his back to Adam, the father of *all* nations.[57]

Jesus showed honor to various groups of people that society deemed lesser citizens. Luke showed that He came to save the paralyzed (Luke 5:17-26), the crippled (13:10-17), the beggar (16:19-31), the little children (18:15-17), and the blind (18:35-43). Numerous times Luke highlighted Jesus' kind treatment of widows (Luke 7:11-17, 18:1-8, 21:1-4). Jesus was exceptionally counter-cultural for His day in how He treated women, allowing their financial involvement in His ministry (Luke 8:1-3) and allowing them to "'sit at his feet' as a learner, just like any other disciple (Luke 10:38-42)."[58] A "sinful woman" was honored with compassion, salvation, and the opportunity to anoint Jesus' feet while at the house of one of the Pharisees (Luke 7:36-50). Luke showed that Jesus came for those society had forgotten.

Luke also placed a high emphasis on Jesus as the Savior for the Gentiles. Luke records a prophetic song that was given through the Holy Spirit to Zechariah, the father of John the Baptist. It was a Messianic song that alluded to the Abrahamic covenant by saying the Messiah came "to show mercy to our ancestors and to remember his holy covenant, the oath he swore to our father Abraham" (Luke 1:72-73). That oath, as we know, stated that "*all peoples on earth* will be blessed" through the descendants of Abraham (Gen 12:1-3, emphasis added). The Jews had become very prideful in their chosenness as Abraham's sons and daughters; however, Luke showed John the Baptist declaring in chapter three verse eight that God "does not need physical offspring. Apart from repentance, one's physical descent from Abraham is valueless."[59] This was a harsh reality for the Jews of Jesus' day, but it once again emphasized that salvation had come for *all* people.

In chapter four, Luke began his portrayal of Jesus' ministry with a story that highlighted the fact that God's salvation was not just for the Jewish people. Jesus was teaching in the synagogue of His hometown when the scroll of Isaiah was handed to Him. It said:

> **The Spirit of the Lord is on me, because he has anointed me to proclaim good news to the poor. He has sent me to proclaim**

---

[57] Craig A. Evans, *Luke*. (Grand Rapids, MI: Baker Publishing Group, 2011), 53.

[58] Elwell and Yarbrough, *Encountering the New Testament*, 89.

[59] Robert H. Stein, *Luke*, vol. 24, *The New American Commentary* (Nashville, TN: B&H Publishing Group, 1992), 133.

> freedom for the prisoners and recovery of sight for the blind, to set the oppressed free, to proclaim the year of the Lord's favor (Luke 4:18-19; Is. 61:1-2, 58:6).

After reading this, He declared that this had been fulfilled in their hearing. This would have been a very bold statement. Yet, "All spoke well of him and were amazed at the gracious words that came from his lips" (Luke 4:22). He then proceeded to share stories of miracles done by both the prophets Elijah and Elisha to non-Israelites. He said:

> I assure you that there were many widows in Israel in Elijah's time, when the sky was shut for three and a half years and there was a severe famine throughout the land. Yet Elijah was not sent to any of them, but to a widow in Zarephath in the region of Sidon. And there were many in Israel with leprosy in the time of Elisha the prophet, yet not one of them was cleansed—only Naaman the Syrian (Luke 4:25-27).

The story about the widow and Elijah (vv. 25-26) refers to the story in 1 Kings chapter seventeen about a non-Israelite widow from Sidon who received the blessing of the Lord. The second story (v. 27) refers to the story in 2 Kings chapter five that was mentioned earlier about Naaman the Syrian. Jesus had the gall to highlight the fact that a non-Israelite Syrian received the blessing of the Lord. He was showing the Israelites that God's purpose was to bless people from Sidon and Syria. He was telling them, contrary to their understanding, that the blessing of the Lord was not just for the Israelites.

They got the message loud and clear, but they did not like it. Their feedback quickly turned from amazement to enragement. After He challenged their supernationalist misunderstanding of the purpose of their chosenness, "All the people in the synagogue were furious when they heard this. They got up, drove him out of the town, and took him to the brow of the hill on which the town was built, in order to throw him off the cliff. But he walked right through the crowd and went on his way" (Luke 4:28-30). He was reminding them of their purpose that they not only had not been able to fulfill, but as time went on, had forgotten entirely. Cornell Goerner says, "No more dramatic illustration could have been given to demonstrate that the grace of God was not limited to the people of Israel and that Gentiles often displayed greater faith than those who were considered 'children of the kingdom.'"[60] Jesus came to fulfill Israel's purpose of blessing all people on earth and redeeming people from all nations, but that message was not well-received by many of the religious elite in Israel.

In chapter eleven, Luke shared the story of the Sign of Jonah. In it, Jesus said that Ninevites (Gentiles) and the Queen of the South would rise at the judgment and condemn the Israelites (Luke 11:29-32). Remember, we have already discussed these two stories from the Old Testament. Jonah was the prophet reluctant to bring a word of salvation to the Ninevites. Then the Ninevites ended up showing more faith and quicker repentance than his own people. The Queen of the South is the Queen of Sheba, who came from afar because of king Solomon's reputation, and she left singing the praises of Yahweh. Jesus was declaring once again that salvation had come for all nations. Elwell and Yarbrough go further to say that they (the Ninevites and the Queen of the south) "will put Israel to shame because of their spiritual discernment."[61]

In chapter seven, Luke showed Jesus commending the faith of a Roman centurion even above the faith of Israel (Luke 7:1-10). In chapter eight, Jesus healed the demoniac of the Gerasenes. The Gerasenes was a Gentile area, validated by the presence of pig farmers. Pigs were unclean animals under the Law of Moses so Israelites would not have been farming them. Luke also shared Jesus' story of the "good" Samaritan, a concept entirely foreign to the Jews of that day and a parable unique to Luke (10:25-37). Chapter seventeen highlights another "good" Samaritan. After Jesus cleansed ten lepers, only one returned to thank him. Luke recorded Jesus saying, "Has no one returned to give praise to God except this foreigner?" (Luke 17:18)

Lastly, the cleansing of the temple is a story that appears in all four of the gospels. "On reaching Jerusalem, Jesus entered the temple courts and began driving out those who were buying and selling there ... 'Is it not written: "My house will be called a house of prayer for all nations"? But you have made it a 'den of robbers'" (Mark 11:15, 17). When Jesus drove out the moneychangers, He was quoting from

---

[60] H. Cornell Goerner, "Jesus and the Gentiles," in *Perspectives on the World Christian Movement: A Reader* (Pasadena, CA: William Carey Library, 2009), 115.

[61] Elwell and Yarbrough, *Encountering the New Testament*, 88.

Isaiah when He said, "For my house will be a house of prayer for all nations" (Is. 56:7). The area that was occupied by the moneychangers was "the Court of the Gentiles, the outer court that Gentiles were allowed to enter."[62] It was the only place in the temple where ceremonially unclean Gentiles could come worship Yahweh. By occupying this space, they were not simply making it a "den of robbers" (Luke 19:46, Jer. 7:11) by profiting off of the devoted followers there to sacrifice to the Lord. They were actually prohibiting the Gentiles from being able to worship God in the temple. Foreigners had had a place of worship in God's temple since the dedication of Solomon's temple (1 Ki. 8:41-43). Jesus' righteous anger came when He saw firsthand that not only were the Israelites not doing what God had set them apart to do, they were now actually prohibiting it from being done at all.

Jesus came as the long-anticipated Messiah to the Jews; however, He did not only come for them. He came so that they might re-engage in God's mission of reconciling the whole earth to Himself. When asked by His disciples when the end of the age would come, He said, "This gospel of the kingdom will be proclaimed as a testimony *to all nations* and then the end will come" (Matt. 24:14, emphasis added). All nations must first hear about God's great love for them. The end of the age will not come until that has happened.

THREE: THE KINGDOM HAS COME

The kingdom Jesus ushered in is a complicated idea and not at all what the Israelites were expecting. They wanted the glory days of David and Solomon's kingdom to return. Even though Jesus came as the One who would sit on their throne for all of eternity, the kingdom He ushered in was a vastly different type of kingdom. This new type of kingdom had more to do with being in relationship with the King Himself. The kingdom of God is not equated with the nation of Israel. It is also not equated with the Church. George Eldon Ladd describes it as this: When the Bible is discussing the kingdom of God, kingdom "always refers to His reign, His rule and His sovereignty. It does not refer to the realm or the geography over which He reigns. David understood this when he said, "The

---

[62] Elwell and Yarbrough, *Encountering the New Testament*, 79.

Lord has established His throne in the heavens, and His Kingdom rules over all" (Ps. 103:19). God's Kingdom is His universal rule, His sovereignty over all the earth. "They shall speak of the glory of Your Kingdom and tell of Your power" (Ps. 145:11)."[63] It is not any geography on earth or in heaven but rather, His reign and Kingship in relationship with His people.

Ladd also says:

> The Kingdom of God is His kingship, His rule, His authority. When we realize this, we can see this meaning in passage after passage in the New Testament. We can see that the Kingdom of God is not a *realm* or a *people*, but it is God's reign. Jesus said that we must "receive the Kingdom of God" as little children (Mark 10:15). What is received? The church? Heaven? What is received is God's rule. In order to enter the future *realm* of the Kingdom, people must submit themselves to God's *rule* here and now.[64]

Therefore, when Jesus spoke about the kingdom of God, He was referring to people from every nation, tribe, and tongue submitting to God's rule on earth. It is a picture of Eden before the fall, living in freedom and victory over evil through submission to the authority of God. It is not simply "inviting Jesus into your heart," to use the popular Christian colloquial saying. It is truly making Him the Lord of your life. It is not simply following the rules because you are supposed to. Rather, it is recognizing that the Law of God is a gift and living in humble submission to it brings life.

In order to illustrate this principle, let's look at some of Jesus' parables. He often taught in parables, some that were obvious in their meaning but many that were not. Keep in mind that most of His parables were very counter-cultural in first-century Palestine. Luke shared one about the kingdom of God being like a great banquet (Luke 14:15-24). A man

---

[63] George Eldon Ladd, "The Gospel of the Kingdom," in *Perspectives on the World Christian Movement: A Reader* (Pasadena, CA: William Carey Library, 2009), 84.
[64] Ibid.

prepared a great banquet and invited all of his friends and family. "But they all alike began to make excuses" (Luke 14:18). So, the man sent out a second round of invitations to those society deemed unworthy, "the poor, the crippled, the blind and the lame" (Luke 14:21). When they still did not fill the table, a third round of invitations were sent out.

Robert Stein calls this "The Great Reversal."[65] Matthew also shared this parable, but Luke's version was unique in that it showed a third sending out of invites, which Stein says, "speaks of the entrance of the Gentiles into God's kingdom."[66] Stein goes on to say that "the rejection of Jesus and the kingdom by official Judaism (14:24) precipitated the inclusion of Israel's outcasts and Gentiles."[67] Israel had been waiting for their Messiah to restore the greatness of their earthly kingdom. Yet, that was never God's intention. His intention was to fulfill the original mission of bringing redemption and relationship to *all* people. He wanted to restore the broken relationships between Himself and mankind, between man and woman, and between man and creation, but that could only happen through His lordship in the lives of all people.

When Jesus said that "the kingdom has come near" (Matt. 10:7), He was saying "The Kingdom of God is here, but instead of destroying human sovereignty, it has attacked the ruling power of Satan. The Kingdom of God is here; but instead of making changes in the external, political order of things, it is making changes in the spiritual order and in the lives of men and women."[68] Jesus said, "The coming of the Kingdom of God is not something that can be observed, nor will people say, 'Here it is,' or 'There it is,' because the Kingdom of God is in your midst" (Luke 17:20-21). When He taught His disciples to pray "Your kingdom come, your will be done, on earth as it is in heaven" (Matt. 6:10), He was telling them (and us) that the internal reign of the King in our lives is contingent on our prayers welcoming Him into loving authority over all aspects of our lives.

---

[65] Stein, *Luke*, 49-50.
[66] Ibid., 394.
[67] Ibid.
[68] Ladd, "The Gospel of the Kingdom," 86-87.

By doing that, each and every person and church becomes a small picture of the ideal Israel. Not a replacement of Israel but rather, as the apostle Peter would later say, "You are a chosen people, a royal priesthood, a holy nation, God's special possession, that you may declare the praises of him who called you out of darkness into his wonderful light. Once you were not a people, but now you are the people of God" (1 Peter 2:9). Does that wording sound familiar? It should. That wording mimics the wording that God used when He choose His chosen nation in Exodus 19. As Israel had been chosen as kingdom-carriers, so now the Church and the individual follower of Jesus have *also* been chosen.

FOUR: AUTHORITY TO GO

Jesus' last appearance on earth, as told in the gospel of Luke, was when He opened the minds of His disciples "so that they could understand the Scriptures" (Luke 24:45). Once their minds were open, Jesus showed them how His death and resurrection were the fulfillment of Old Testament prophecies. When He said, "This is what is written" in verse 46, He was not quoting one specific prophecy but instead the "entire Old Testament teaching on this."[69] Luke emphasized that Jesus was the fulfillment. In further fulfillment of Old Testament prophecy, Jesus then commissioned His followers to preach the message of repentance and salvation *to all nations* (Luke 24:47, emphasis added).

The nation of Israel had been given a specific mission: be a blessing to all peoples of the earth. Idolatry and disobedience kept them from fulfilling their mission, so Jesus was sent to usher in a new way. It is important to keep in mind that God still intended on doing it through His chosen nation Israel. Israel was not neglected or forgotten or disregarded. From Israel came the Messiah, the Davidic King, who would rule for all of eternity. He did not come first for the Gentiles but rather, He came in order that God's mission could finally be accomplished *through* Israel.

---

[69] Stein, *Luke*, 620.

As we saw earlier, Jesus started with the twelve, who were a picture of the twelve tribes of Jacob/Israel. They were multiplied to the seventy-two, who were a picture of the nations. In the only instance in Scripture where it says, "and then the end will come" (Matt. 24:14b), Jesus commissioned His followers to fulfill Israel's original mission. He said, "This gospel of the kingdom will be preached in the whole world as a testimony to all nations, and then the end will come" (Matt. 24:14). Mark recorded the same commission in the context of what to expect in the end times and said, "The gospel must first be preached to all nations" (Mark 13:10). The message of God's kingdom reign on earth must be shared with all peoples of the earth. Redemption, salvation, and relationship with the King must be proclaimed to *all nations* before the inevitable return of Christ and end of the present age. God's mission, which He first gave to Israel, must be completed. "And then the end will come" (Matt. 24:14).

This is often called the Great Commission. Many Christians are familiar with that phrase from Matthew's gospel. After Christ's death and resurrection, before He returned to Heaven, He said, "All authority in heaven and on earth has been given to me. Therefore go and make disciples of all nations, baptizing them in the name of the Father and of the Son and of the Holy Spirit, and teaching them to obey everything I have commanded you. And surely I am with you always, to the very end of the age" (Matt. 28:18-20). Unfortunately, many Christians have taken this as only applicable to those who are called to be career missionaries in faraway lands. That could not be further from the truth. This is the summation of God's mission from the beginning. When He blessed mankind and then gave the very first command in Genesis 1:28, saying, "Be fruitful and increase in number; fill the earth and subdue it," He was declaring His desire to fill the earth with those who bore His image and reflected His glory. This has been His purpose since the beginning of time. The redemption plan implemented through the descendants of Abraham was meant to fulfill this purpose. Now the followers of Jesus have been brought into God's great redemption plan.

Matthew is not the only gospel account that included this commissioning statement. In fact, all four gospels and the book of Acts include a similar statement. Mark recorded Jesus as saying, "Go into all the world and preach the gospel to all creation. Whoever believes and is baptized will be saved, but whoever does not believe will be condemned" (Mark 16:15-16). God was not condemning them. The world was already condemned and consumed by sin, idolatry, hatred, and death. God was making a way, a straight path to redemption, "a way in the wilderness" (Is. 40:3; 43:19; Mark 1:3). Luke said, "Repentance for the forgiveness of sins will be preached in [Jesus'] name to all nations, beginning at Jerusalem" (Luke 24:47). Again, it started with Israel. It started in Jerusalem and would go out to all the nations.

John said that Jesus prayed for His disciples and said to the Lord, "As you sent me into the world, I have sent them into the world" (John 17:18). How was Jesus sent into the world? John says, "No one has ever seen God, but the one and only Son, who is himself God and is in closest relationship with the Father, has made him known" (John 1:18). Jesus came to make God *known*. Then He prayed that His disciples would do the same. Go into the world and make Him *known* among the nations. Jesus did not come to condemn, for the world had already been condemned since the fall of man in Genesis chapter three. Jesus was the one foreshadowed that day, the One who would crush the head of the enemy (Gen. 3:15). Jesus came that God might save the world through Him (John 3:16-18).

Finally, the book of Acts begins with Jesus' final commissioning to His followers. They asked Him again, "Are you at this time going to restore the kingdom to Israel?" (Acts 1:6) They were still trying to understand the kingdom that Jesus was ushering in. Jesus said that was not for them to know *but*—on the contrary to that—instead of what they were actually expecting, He said, "But you will receive power when the Holy Spirit comes on you; and you will be my witnesses in Jerusalem, and in all Judea and Samaria, and to the ends of the earth" (Acts 1:8). The restoration of Israel's earthly kingdom was not the right question. Jesus was commissioning His followers to the mission of God that had been given to Israel and was now also being given to the Church. But this time, the mission came with a different expression of supernatural power for its completion.

FIVE: DEATH AND RESURRECTION

Mark's gospel is unique in that it seems to emphasis the passion of Christ through His suffering, death, and resurrection more than the other gospels. He records Jesus saying that the kingdom of God would come with power (Mark 9:1). That power would be the indwelling Holy Spirit. In order to understand that and why Jesus had to die, we need to return to the Old Testament. Remember the marriage ceremony of God and His beloved Israel at the base of Mount Sinai? Before God's presence came down the mountain, He told Moses to have the people consecrate themselves (Ex. 19:10-11). On the third day, He would come down, but they first had to be consecrated. Strong's concordance defines the word "consecrate" as to sanctify, to prepare, and to make holy.[70] In order to be in the presence of a Holy God, the people had to be sanctified and made holy themselves. In the same way, before God's Holy Presence came into the tabernacle, the priests who were responsible for it had to be consecrated (Ex. 40:12-15). God's Presence could not come among unholy and unsanctified people.

When the ark of the Lord was brought to Jerusalem, "the priests and Levites consecrated themselves" (1 Chron. 15:14). God gave David specific instructions for building the temple so that it would be sanctified for His presence (1 Chron. 22, 28 – 29). Even the builders of the temple were asked "Now, who among you is willing to consecrate yourself to the Lord today?" (1 Chron. 29:5) When the temple was finished, Solomon dedicated it to the Lord and "all the priests who were there had consecrated themselves, regardless of their divisions" (2 Chron. 5:11). God's Holy Presence could not rest among the unholy, but His desire from the beginning of creation was to dwell among His creation (Gen. 3:8a). He wanted His Spirit to reside in the midst of His people. This was shown in the building of the tabernacle in the wilderness and then the building of the temple in Jerusalem. In fact, the word "tabernacle" means dwelling place. But in order for His Presence to dwell, they had to be made holy. Eventually when the Israelites became unholy, God's Presence left.

---

[70] "6942. Qadash," *BibleHub.com*, 2024, https://biblehub.com/hebrew/6942.htm.

The temple was the pride and joy of Israel because the Spirit of the Lord resided in it. However, the Presence of the Lord had not returned to the temple, even after it was rebuilt in post-exilic Israel. Until Jesus came. When Mary and Joseph took the young Jesus to Jerusalem "to present him to the Lord (as it is written in the Law of the Lord, "Every firstborn male is to be consecrated to the Lord")" (Luke 2:22-23; Ex. 13:2, 12), the Presence of the Lord returned to the temple for the first time in centuries. And Simeon declared, "For my eyes have seen your salvation, which you have prepared in the sight of all nations; a light for revelation to the Gentiles, and the glory of your people Israel" (Luke 2:30-32). Jesus was the Presence of God returning to Israel.

Jesus undoubtedly returned to the temple multiple times throughout His lifetime, some of which are recorded in the gospels. When John recorded the story of Jesus going to Jerusalem for the Jewish Passover festival, he shared the story of Jesus clearing out the temple courts. "His disciples remembered that it is written: 'Zeal for your house will consume me'" (John 2:17; Ps. 69:9). There was no doubt in their minds that He felt the same way about the temple as the rest of Israel. As the psalmist had said, "How lovely is your dwelling place, Lord Almighty!" (Ps. 84:1) and "Within your temple, O God, we meditate on your unfailing love" (Ps. 48:9). The temple was the closest that they could come to the Lord. In what would have been a shocking statement, Jesus said, "Destroy this temple, and I will raise it again in three days" (John 2:19). The religious elite probably laughed and scoffed at such a ridiculous statement because it had taken forty-six years to build that temple (John 2:20). But the temple Jesus spoke about was both literal and figurative. The temple He spoke of was His own body (John 2:21). While the temple in Jerusalem no longer housed the Spirit of God, His body did.

The Spirit of God had come upon Him at His baptism (Matt. 3:16). He was the walking, talking, breathing Temple of God. Isaiah had prophesied about this, saying, "Here is my servant, whom I uphold, my chosen one whom I delight; I will put my Spirit on him, and he will bring justice to the nations" (Is. 42:1). Jesus also said that the physical temple in Jerusalem would literally be destroyed (Matt. 24:1-2; Mark 13:1-2). The physical temple was, in fact, destroyed shortly after His death and resurrection. In 70 A.D., the Romans squelched a military uprising from the Jews, scattering them from the land and bringing their beloved temple to ruin. To this day there remains only a fragment of the temple in Jerusalem.

However sad that day must have been, the temple was no longer needed to house the Spirit of God because He had a new dwelling place: the believer. Jesus had told His followers that the Father would send the Holy Spirit in Jesus' place (John 14:26). He said it was better that He leave so that the Holy Spirit might come (John 16:7). The Holy Spirit would glorify Jesus through His followers (John 16:13-15). Consider this: God set out to accomplish His mission through the nation of Israel through the power of His Presence that dwelled among them. Then, His Spirit dwelled within His Son, Jesus, empowering Him to be His Servant and accomplish His mission. Finally, God sent His Holy Spirit to dwell among the individuals who choose to follow Jesus and therefore make up the Church so that they could be His "witnesses in Jerusalem, and Judea and Samaria, and to the ends of the earth" (Acts 1:8). The instrument of blessing and carrier of His Presence changed, but the power and purpose never did.

How could His Holy Presence dwell among mere mortals, though? Only through Jesus. When Jesus took our sin upon Himself, He consecrated us. His atoning sacrifice made the way for us to be pure and holy and blameless. The writer of Hebrews talks about how "the first covenant was not put into effect without blood" (Heb. 9:18). The blood of the cutting of the covenant between Abraham and God, the blood of the Passover lamb in Egypt, the blood of the sacrifices required to purify Israel. Moses had sprinkled the people with the blood of the sacrifices and said, "This is the blood of the covenant, which God has commanded you to keep" (Heb. 9:20; Ex. 24:8). "In the same way, he sprinkled with the blood both the tabernacle and everything used in its ceremonies. In fact, the law requires that nearly everything be cleansed with blood, and without the shedding of blood there is no forgiveness" (Heb. 9:21-22). Isaiah said about the Suffering Servant, who was the coming Messiah, "So he will sprinkle the nations" (Is. 52:15). The sprinkling of the blood of the sacrifices consecrated the tabernacle for His Holy Presence. The sprinkling of the blood of Jesus' sacrifice consecrated the new tabernacle. Because of this, "we have confidence to enter the Most Holy Place," which was the specific place within the temple where God's Presence dwelled, "by the blood of Jesus" (Heb. 10:19). It is His sacrifice that made us clean. It was only because of this that His Spirit could tabernacle within us. Now each person that has been sanctified by the blood of Christ is the walking, talking, breathing Temple of God (1 Corin. 6:19).

During the period of time leading up to Judah's exile to Babylon, the prophet Jeremiah lamented their circumstances, saying, "How the precious children of Zion, once worth their weight in gold, are now considered as pots of clay" (Lam. 4:2). What had once been precious became commonplace, simple earthen jars. But through the atoning sacrifice of Jesus, we who were once commonplace have become precious. We now have a treasure within our common and humble beings. These jars of clay are our very own bodies, and they now hold precious treasure inside (2 Corin. 4:7). Within these once ceremonially unclean vessels is the very Presence and Glory of God. Christ's salvific death and resurrection is not just about where we go when we die. It enables us to carry the Glory of God within us as we participate in what God has been doing since the beginning of time. Filling the earth with those who bear His image and reflect His glory *so that* all peoples on earth can be blessed with the same blessing we have received.

The New Covenant

THE JEW OF JEWS

The apostle Paul is credited with writing most of the New Testament. Thirteen of the books in the New Testament are epistles, or letters, that Paul wrote to individuals and to churches. He was once the main protagonist in the anti-Jesus movement, pursuing and killing many of the followers of Jesus (Acts 8:1-3). His passion and zeal for his Jewish beliefs led him in his murderous quest to purge the land of what he believed was apostasy and false teaching. Then, he met the Messiah on the road to Damascus and that encounter changed the trajectory of his life and that of the Church (Acts 9).

If you look up that story in your Bible, it might be listed under the subtitle of "Saul's Conversion." (Saul was his Hebrew name and for reasons debated by scholars, he began referring to himself by his Greek name, Paul, in Acts 13:6.) Scripture is inerrant and divinely inspired, but the subtitles, chapter divisions, and verse numbers are not. That being said, calling Paul's encounter on the road to Damascus a "conversion" is simply not accurate. Paul never denounced Judaism; he simply met the foretold Jewish Messiah and followed Him. Throughout his letters, he goes to great lengths to show that regardless of what happened to him on the road to Damascus, he never abandoned Judaism. He still cared deeply for "his people," the people of Israel, to the point of even wishing himself "cursed and cut off from Christ for the sake of [them]" (Rom 9:2-4). According to Mark D. Nanos, "Acts emphasizes that Paul remained a [Jewish leader] and practiced Torah and temple sacrifices (cf. Acts 21:23-26)."[71] Nanos also says, "In keeping with Paul's understanding from Scripture, Israel's special trust is to receive and declare God's Word among the nations."[72] Paul understood the Abrahamic Covenant and Israel's role in reconciling the nations to God. Therefore, when he was *called* on the Damascus road, he did not *abandon* Judaism in order to advocate for the Gentiles' inclusion in God's covenant. He simply began walking in the purpose God had established for the Israelites hundreds of years prior. This is why many Jewish followers of Jesus today refer to themselves as "completed Jews" over the more historically common "Messianic Jew." Either title properly connotes not a conversion, but a continuation from ancient Judaism to following Jesus.

Paul called himself "a Hebrew of Hebrews" in his letter to the church in Philippi. He said of himself that he was "circumcised on the eighth day, of the people of Israel, of the tribe of Benjamin, a Hebrew of Hebrews; in regard to the law, a Pharisee; as for zeal, persecuting the church; as for righteousness based on the law, faultless" (Phil. 3:5-6). He was the most Jewish Jew that there was, and he prided himself in that. Yet even for him, following Christ was not abandoning Judaism. Everything that he wrote on the subject affirms that he truly believed that following Christ was not a new religion, but rather, the fulfillment of his Jewish beliefs. He did not inherit a new purpose when he began following Christ. Rather, he finally understood his purpose, which had been the purpose of Israel since before Israel existed when God called Abraham.

Paul saw the new covenant truly as an extension of the old covenant, not a replacement of it. He said, "Understand, then, that those who have faith are children of Abraham. Scripture foresaw that God would justify the Gentiles by faith, and announced *the gospel* in advance to Abraham:

---

[71] Mark D. Nanos, "A Jewish Perspective," in *Four Views on the Apostle Paul*, ed. Michael F. Bird, (Grand Rapids, MI: Zondervan, 2012), 174.

[72] Ibid., 167.

'All nations will be blessed through you'" (Gal. 3:7-8, emphasis added). Do not miss that Paul called the Abrahamic Covenant "the gospel!" Then he said, "[Christ] redeemed us in order that the blessing given to Abraham might come to the Gentiles through Christ Jesus, so that by faith we might receive the promise of the Spirit" (Gal. 3:14). The blessing given to Abraham, which was that all nations would be blessed with a redemptive relationship with God, came to the Gentiles. "So in Christ Jesus you are all children of God through faith ... There is neither Jew nor Gentile ... for you are all one in Christ Jesus. If you belong to Christ, then you are Abraham's seed, and heirs according to the promise" (Gal. 3:26, 28-29). This is what following Christ meant for Paul. He did not "convert" to Christianity. Following Christ was simply the continuation of his faithful devotion to Yahweh.

Jesus had said to the religious elite, "Your father Abraham rejoiced at the thought of seeing my day; he saw it and was glad" (John 8:56). Paul understood this. In a very informal interview, N.T. Wright, a well-known Pauline scholar, said this in relation to people's perception of Paul as a Jew:

> The normal narrative, and I've heard it again and again, is that well the Jewish thing was that God had ... a first shot at making people alright by calling Abraham and giving Moses the law but that somehow didn't work. So, He said we'll scrap that and send Jesus instead. Whereas for Paul, and this is what I think people don't really know, for Paul, Jesus comes precisely as *the fulfillment of the Israel project*, in order to get the human project relaunched ... Because humans are God's means of working in and for the world, Israel was His means of rescuing humans so it's a kind of chain reaction. Until you see it like that, there's all sorts of bits of Paul which ... won't quite join up and make much sense.[73]

In other words, when the Church does not understand God's mission in the world and His purpose for Israel, much of what Paul said will not make sense. Because Old Testament illiteracy runs rampant in the American Church, Christians continue to argue about Paul's teachings because

---

[73] Faith Adjacent podcast (Oct 19, 2023. Quote shortened for succinctness and understanding)

outside of the grand narrative context, some of them simply do not make sense. Knowing now the purpose of it all perhaps changes one's perception of what Paul meant in his letter to the Roman Church when he was sharing his anguish over Israel. He said:

> It is not as though God's word had failed. For *not all who are descended from Israel are Israel. Nor because they are his descendants are they all Abraham's children.* On the contrary, "It is through Isaac that your offspring will be reckoned." In other words, it is not the children by physical descent who are God's children, but it is the children of the promise who are regarded as Abraham's offspring (Rom. 9:6-8, emphasis added).

It is not the children by physical descent, but children of the promise. Children of the covenant. Children who are willing to be a part of what God is doing in the world through them, to bring the nations into a redeemed relationship with the One True God. "What if he did this to make the riches of his glory known to the objects of his mercy, whom he prepared in advance for glory – even us, whom he also called, not only from the Jews but also from the Gentiles?" (Rom. 9:23-24). Indeed, what if He did?

For Paul, as it should be for us, it is not a matter of Israel *or* the Church. It is both. Paul asked the question, "Did God reject his people? By no means!" (Rom. 11:1) Then later in that chapter he asked the rhetorical question of whether or not Israel had stumbled beyond recovery, to which he answers, "Not at all!" (Rom. 11:11). There is a section in his letter to the church in Ephesus that explains this a little better. He says to the Gentiles about their pre-Christ circumstances, "Remember that at that time you were separate from Christ, excluded from citizenship in Israel and foreigners to the covenants of the promise, without hope and without God in the world. But now in Christ Jesus you who once were far away have been brought near by the blood of Christ" (Eph. 2:12-13). Israel had not pursued their mission to the Gentiles and had not treated the foreigner among them in the way that the Lord had instructed them. Where Israel failed to make a way for them, Christ succeeded in bringing them near to God. But there is more.

Paul then says Jesus "is our peace, who has made the two groups one and has destroyed the barrier, the dividing wall of hostility … His purpose was to create in himself one new humanity out of the two, thus making peace, and in one body to reconcile both of them to God through the cross, by which he put to death their hostility. He came and preached peace to you who were far away and peace to those who were near. For through him we both have access to the Father by one Spirit" (Eph. 2:14-18). Imagine that. Imagine Israel *and* the Church working together through the power of the Holy Spirit to bring peace and salvation to those who are far from God!

The Gentiles did not *replace* Israel in God's sentiments or mission. The Church did not *replace* Israel. The Church, according to Paul, is composed not of foreigners and strangers to God and His covenant but rather, the Church is made up of "fellow citizens with God's people and also members of his household" (Eph. 2:19). The foundation of this joint household is the apostles (new covenant) and the prophets (old covenant), "with Christ Jesus himself as the chief cornerstone. In him the whole building is joined together and rises to become a *holy temple* in the Lord … a dwelling in which God lives by his Spirit" (Eph 2:20-22). Did Jesus not say that His "Father's house has many rooms?" (John 14:2). The Church did not take over the building. The Church simply got to move in alongside Israel.

The mystery of the prophets of old is that "through the gospel the Gentiles are heirs together with Israel, members together of one body, and sharers together in the promise of Christ Jesus" (Eph. 3:6). Elwell and Yarbrough state, "None of this excludes the importance of Israel (Luke 1:30-33), but it does broaden the idea of Israel's blessedness by presenting it as *the means of God's mercy reaching all nations, not just Abraham's descendants.*"[74] It is a picture of the fulfillment of the Abrahamic Covenant, that the nation of Israel would be the conduit of blessing for all nations.

---

[74] Elwell and Yarbrough, *Encountering the New Testament*, 88. Emphasis added.

FATHERHOOD AND ADOPTION

When I first started asking the questions that God had put on my heart and mind that eventually led to this writing, some people would be quick to exclaim, "That's replacement theology!" That exclamation typically came with the tone of an accusation of apostasy. I hope at this point it is clear that I am not advocating for the idea that the Church has replaced Israel. I do not believe that. I do think there is a blind spot in our theology that keeps the western Church from understanding the relationship between Israel and the Church.

Often Christians have the assumption that Israel was the natural-born son and that the Church was then adopted, so to speak, and grafted in. Russell Moore rightly points out in his book titled *Adopted for Life* that this is an incorrect assumption. He says:

> Paul says that Israel was adopted too (Rom. 9:4). Of course, God once said, "Your origin and your birth are of the land of the Canaanites; your father was an Amorite and your mother a Hittite" (Ezek. 16:3). The Israelites were once Gentiles too. God reminds Israel that he "found him in a desert land, and in the howling waste of the wilderness" (Deut. 32:10). Israel was an abandoned baby, wallowing in its own blood on the roadside (Ezek. 16:5).[75]

We were all orphans until God found us, whether in Egypt as slaves, first century Palestine as slaves, or twenty-first century America as slaves. Slaves to the law, to sin, to death, to idolatry, and to hopelessness. Until God came and rescued us. He then gave us His Spirit, first in the tabernacle, then in the temple, now in the body of the believer. "The Spirit you received brought about your adoption to sonship. And by him we cry, '*Abba*, Father.' The Spirit himself testifies with our spirit that we are God's children" (Rom. 8:15-16). Have you ever met that family at church that has adopted children from all over the world? I feel like most churches have at least one. Perhaps they are a middle-class, American Caucasian couple with children of African, Asian, and Indian descent. Their family

---

[75] Russell Moore, *Adopted for Life* (Wheaton, IL; Crossway, 2015), 26.

looks like a beautiful picture of humanity. That is what God's family looks like. His family is not all Jewish. His family is not all western Christian. God's family is representative of the beauty and uniqueness of every nation, tribe, and tongue on earth. All of them were adopted out of slavery into sonship as joint heirs with the "one and only Son" of God, who is Christ Jesus (John 3:16; Rom. 8:17).

Jackson W. discusses this idea of adoption into sonship in his book *Reading Romans with Eastern Eyes*. In reference to Romans chapter four, Paul is addressing the question of who the "descendants of Abraham" are. Jackson says, "[Paul] overwhelmingly emphasizes that Abraham is the father of all by faith, whether circumcised (Jews) or uncircumcised (Gentiles). In short, Paul refutes the idea that Abraham is father only to the Jews 'according to the flesh.' He answers 'no' to the question posed in Romans 4:1."[76] Abraham was not justified by works or by natural sonship but rather by faith (Rom. 4:3; Gen. 15:6). David also "speaks of the blessedness of those to whom God credits righteousness apart from works" (Rom. 4:6). Therefore, the promise and blessing of God "comes by faith… not only to those who are of the law but also to those who have *the faith* of Abraham. He is the father of us all" (Rom. 4:16, emphasis added).

When God told Abraham that He would bless his descendants and that "all peoples on earth will be blessed" through them (Gen. 12:2-3), that blessing and purpose applies to all of the children of Abraham. The Abrahamic covenant is, therefore, no longer God's covenant *only* with Israel. It is the new covenant as well, brought to the Gentiles through the death and resurrection of Jesus. Jesus redeemed the sins of the world, thus making His followers sons and daughters of the promise and of Abraham, carriers of the Spirit of God, and blessed with redemption in order to bless all peoples on earth.

PURCHASED

Remember that we talked about the sanctifying blood of Jesus and how

---

[76] Jackson W, *Reading Romans with Eastern Eyes* (Downers Grove, IL; InterVarsity, 2019), 87.

it cleansed the dirty unclean vessels from sin in order that the indwelling Holy Spirit might come? Blood was necessary for the covenant and for forgiveness; however, it can be one of the weirder aspects of the Jewish and Christian faith. Painting the doorframe with blood? Sprinkling holy items with blood to clean them? Drinking the metaphorical blood of the new covenant? These are the topics you hope the preacher does not talk about when you bring your unbelieving friends to church or synagogue. It is particularly challenging for those who, like me, are squeamish about blood. For reasons we cannot fully grasp, blood is important to God.

God had said that Abel's blood cried out to him from the ground when Cain murdered him (Gen. 4:10). When He first told Noah to eat meat, He prohibited him from eating any that still had its "lifeblood" in it (Gen. 9:4). Throughout Scripture, blood is shown to hold back God's wrath. Blood is actually quite fascinating if you can set aside the squeamishness. It can be used to diagnose countless health issues. Blood contains DNA markers unique to each person. Each person's blood is as unique as their fingerprints. Not only can a person be identified by a blood sample but there are also genetic markers in the blood that can identify paternity and other family members. There are blood tests that can identify the exact ethnic make-up of a person. When I was pregnant with my third child, a blood test done at eight weeks revealed the gender of my child. Blood is how information passes through the various cells of the body. The creative design of the human body by God is truly fascinating.

However, there is one aspect of blood that is rarely discussed, but it is perhaps one of the most important. In God's economy, blood is currency. Jesus said at the last supper "This is my blood of the covenant, which is poured out for many for the forgiveness of sins" (Matt. 26:28). He asked His disciples to drink from this cup which symbolized His blood (Matt. 26:27). As N.T. Wright says:

> We should note, first, that this meal, like all Jewish Passover meals, celebrated the exodus, Israel's liberation from slavery in Egypt. To the first-century Jew, it also pointed ahead to the return from exile, the new exodus, the great covenant renewal spoken

of by the prophets. The meal symbolized "forgiveness of sins," YHWH's return to redeem his people, his victory over Pharoahs both literal and figurative ... this was the meal, in other words, which said that Israel's God was about to become king.[77]

All four gospel accounts share this story, and they all share some version of "the blood of the covenant." Wright points out that this "echoes the story in which Moses established the first covenant with the people at Mount Sinai."[78] The symbolism here also echoes that moment.

In first-century Palestine, there was a normal, customary practice of a betrothal period that lasted about a year. It was similar to what we in the western world know today as the engagement period, but the betrothal is so much more than just planning a wedding. During the betrothal period, the man and woman were legally bound together and although not technically married yet, a breakup would require a legal divorce (Matt. 1:18-19). The betrothal custom involved the parents of the young man and young woman negotiating the terms of the proposal and the bride price. When an agreement was made, the would-be husband would pour a glass of wine and offer it to his beloved. If she accepted the glass, she was saying yes to his proposal. During that betrothal period, they were legally bound to each other, but they did not live together or consummate the marriage. The bride remained with her parents until the wedding when the bridegroom would return for her.

Recall the marriage symbolism at Mount Sinai, where Yahweh proposed a covenant to His chosen nation. Israel had said yes. At the last supper, Jesus offered the cup to His disciples. In essence, He was doing what God had done to Israel. Jesus was choosing them for the new covenant. He had already referred to Himself as the bridegroom (Matt. 9:15; Mark 2:20; Luke 5:35). The last supper was His official proposal. Once again, the twelve, the picture of Israel, said yes.

At the end of God's story, we can actually see a picture of the completed

---

[77] N. T. Wright, *The New Testament in its World* (Great Britain; Society for Promoting Christian Knowledge, 2019), 253.
[78] Ibid., 254.

Abrahamic Covenant. The covenant made with Abraham, where God said He Himself would shed blood to keep it (Gen. 15). The covenant made with Israel at Mount Sinai, where God said that Israel would be His kingdom of priests (Ex. 19:5-6). The covenant made with David and Solomon, that from them would come a King who would sit on an eternal throne (2 Sam. 7:16; 1 Kings 9:5). The covenant made with the disciples of Jesus in the upper room (Matt. 26:26-28; Mark 14:22-25; Luke 22:14-20). All of the covenants had converged into one, concluding with a beautiful picture of what God had been seeking since creation. The apostle John entered the throne room of heaven by means of a prophetic vision. While there, he saw "the Lion of the tribe of Judah, the Root of David" on the throne, encircled by all of heaven (Rev. 5:5-8). They were all singing a song of worship in which they said:

> You are worthy to take the scroll and to open its seal, because you were slain and with your blood *you purchased for God* members of every tribe and language and people and nations. You have made them to be a kingdom and priests to serve our God, and they will reign on the earth (Rev. 5:9-10, emphasis added).

The bridegroom had purchased for God with His very own blood the fulfillment of all the covenants—worshipers from all the peoples of earth—just as He had said when asked by His disciples when He would return. He would not return until He got everything that He paid for. Isaiah had prophesied about this fulfillment, saying, "They will proclaim my glory among the nations. And they will bring all your people, from all the nations, to my holy mountain in Jerusalem as an offering to the Lord ... They will bring them, as the Israelites bring their grain offerings, to the temple of the Lord in ceremonially clean vessels" (Is. 66:19-20). Ceremonially clean vessels, because of the cleansing blood of Jesus. All nations. All tribes. All languages. All people. Represented around the eternal throne of the True King.

Application for Today

MODERN DAY ISRAEL AND THE COVENANT

Now all of this background information begs the question, what does it all mean for modern day Israel? The nation of Israel was chosen to be the carriers of the Presence of God. God could have picked anyone when He chose Abram. He could have done what He sought to do through Israel using any nation He wanted. It was not Israel that was specially qualified for the mission. It was His presence that made them specially qualified. His choice made them chosen. It was not because of anything they did or believed. He chose them before they did or believed anything. He chose them before they even existed to fulfill His purposes. He could have chosen anyone (Deut. 7:6). It truly is all about His Holy Presence (Ex. 33:15-16).

Many well-meaning people will use the Abrahamic covenant to argue that a curse will come upon anyone who does not stand with modern-day Israel. As we have seen, that covenant includes the Church as well. The Church is not outside of that covenant, but rather a part of it. The promise of blessing or curse, just like the promise of being blessed to be a blessing, is not limited to the modern geo-political nation named Israel. It is for the descendants of Abraham who are walking in the covenant. The Abrahamic Covenant in and of itself does not contain theological grounding that requires every Christian person and/or nation to stand alongside modern-day Israel without question.

Israel of the Old Testament had God's blessing and favor when they were walking in the covenant. When they were not walking in it, they received God's punishment. Proverbs 3:12 says, "The Lord disciplines those he loves, as a father the son he delights in." The writer of Hebrews quoted this proverb, adding "He chastens everyone he accepts as his son" (Heb. 12:6). God's discipline, even His punishment, is for the good of His people and the glory of His name. Certainly, it never seems pleasant at the time it is delivered, but later "it produces a harvest of righteousness" (Heb. 12:11). God promised to always be willing to accept Israel's repentance and their return to the covenant (Deut. 30:1-5). Whenever that happened, God's blessing and favor returned to them.

One would be wise not to automatically equate all of the prophecies about Israel and/or Judah with the modern nation of Israel. There are certainly many prophecies that are fulfilled in part with modern-day Israel. But should we assume that modern-day Israel will be allowed to stay in the land forever if they disregard the covenant? That is up to the Lord. He has removed them from the land multiple times for disobedience to the covenant. That begs another question. Is modern-day Israel walking in obedience to the covenant? These are not antisemitic questions. These are questions warranted in historical events and prophecy. Out of an abundance of caution and clarity, I would like to make it clear that I would love to see the chosen people, whether those living in the land of Israel or those scattered to the ends of the earth, step into the fullness of God's kingdom. Furthermore, I believe that they were once again given special favor and blessing from Yahweh when they returned to the land post World War II. But what exactly does that mean biblically? Let's look with a critical lens at some of the prophecies compared to the modern day geo-political nation of Israel.

One such prophecy came from Jeremiah. He delivered a message about God's judgment coming on Babylon. He said, "Babylon will be captured; Bel will be put to shame, Marduk filled with terror" (Jer. 50:2). Bel and

Marduk were the gods of the Babylonians. Babylon eventually fell to the Persian Empire in 539 B.C. There was a literal fulfillment of this prophecy; however, many people agree that Babylon, though an actual historical nation, is also an archetype of the kingdom of darkness. This is demonstrated in the book of Revelation, which contains multiple references to Babylon. Most scholars agree that Revelation was written somewhere between 81 and 96 A.D. Applying Revelation's prophecy literally to a kingdom that had not existed in over 600 years seems inconsistent with John's intent.

Returning to Jeremiah, after he says that Babylon will fall, he says, "In those times, at that time," declares the Lord, "the people of Israel and the people of Judah together will go in tears to seek the Lord their God. They will ask the way to Zion and turn their faces toward it. They will come and bind themselves to the Lord in an everlasting covenant that will not be forgotten" (Jer. 50:4-5). This is referring to Israel and Judah being reunited. Remember that the kingdom was divided after Solomon's reign. Ezekiel also talked about the reunification of Israel and Judah in chapter thirty-seven. Although theories abound, most people agree that the ten lost tribes of Israel are still lost. In that vein, one could surmise that Jeremiah's prophecy is not yet fulfilled. Even though Babylon the historical nation has been conquered, the kingdom of darkness is still present, and the book of Revelation shows the fall of Babylon as a future event.

Ezekiel said that the Lord would bring Israel back to the land:

> For I will take you out of the nations; I will gather you from all the countries and bring you back into your own land. I will sprinkle clean water on you, and you will be clean; I will cleanse you from all your impurities and from all your idols. I will give you a new heart and put a new spirit in you; I will remove from you your heart of stone and give you a heart of flesh. And *I will put my Spirit in you* and move you to follow my decrees and be careful to keep my laws. Then you will live in the land I gave your ancestors; you will be my people, and I will be your God (Ez. 36:24-28, emphasis added).

Let's unpack this a bit. Modern day Israel began in 1946 when England, who controlled Palestine, allowed some of the land to be a place of refuge and a new home for those Jews who survived the atrocities of World War II and the Holocaust. Two years later, Israel became its own nation. God was saying through Ezekiel that He would, in fact, bring His chosen people back to their own land. Was this prophecy fulfilled in 1946/1948?

Ezekiel used the same verbiage as we previously discussed of Jesus, sprinkling the nations clean (Is. 52:15). Jesus was indeed sent to do this, both for Jew and Gentile; however, the majority of the Jewish people rejected Him (Mark 12:10; Ps. 118:22; Is. 53:3). He was also sent to "put a new spirit in" (Ez. 36:26) and not just any new spirit, *His* Spirit (v. 27a). Jesus did that, cleansing those who believed in Him in order for the indwelling Holy Spirit to come. Ezekiel said this Spirit would "move you to follow my decrees and be careful to keep my laws" (Ez. 36:27b). Jesus said the Holy Spirit was "the Spirit of truth," guiding believers "into all the truth" (John 16:13). He said the Holy Spirit would also "teach you all things and will remind you of everything" He had said (John 14:26). That sounds like the Spirit of God that Ezekiel prophesied about. Ezekiel said after these things happened, "*then* you will live in the land I gave your ancestors; you will be my people, and I will be your God" (Ez. 36:28). The Jewish people, in large part, rejected Jesus as the prophesied Messiah and have not *yet* received the Spirit.

Again, Ezekiel said one chapter later that God would bring the people of Israel back to their own land, making them one nation under one king. This king would be the new David and would rule forever (Ez. 37:15-28). This obviously cannot *yet* apply to modern-day Israel because they are not yet united under the reign of King Jesus. That does not mean that it will not happen. In fact, we know from Scripture that it *will* happen. Israel will recognize Jesus as Messiah. They just have not as a whole done it yet. Perhaps God brought them back into the land in 1946 as another opportunity to repent and walk in the covenant once again. Ironically, Isaiah talked about the nations themselves being the ones to bring Israel into the new covenant. Through Isaiah, the Lord said, "See, I will beckon to the nations, I will lift up my banner to the peoples; they will bring your sons in their arms and carry your daughters on their hips" (Is. 49:22). Paul said that "Israel has experienced a hardening in part until the full measure of the Gentiles has come in" (Rom. 11:25) and then all Israel will be saved. Israel is still loved by God "on account of the patriarchs" (Rom. 11:28) but they were not walking in the covenant in the first century, and the vast majority are still not today.

Jeremiah said in chapter eleven that Israel and Judah were cursed when they broke the covenant (Jer. 11:1-4, 10). God said that because they did not keep the covenant, He brought all of the curses upon them that He had warned them would come (Jer. 11:8). Then, in a shocking statement of righteous anger, God said, "Do not pray for this people or offer any plea or petition for them, because I will not listen when they call to me in the time of their distress" (Jer. 11:14). In chapter twenty-three, however, He says that the Messiah would save Judah and Israel. "The days are coming … when I will raise up for David a righteous Branch, a King who will reign wisely and do what is just and right in the land. In his days Judah will be saved and Israel will live in safety" (Jer. 23: 5-6). Then a new covenant would come through the Messiah. It would not be like the old covenant because they broke it (Jer. 31:32). God's law would be written on their minds and hearts and the whole world would know the God of Israel (Jer. 31:33-34).

Are they walking in the covenant now? According to recent data, at least 40% of modern Israelis consider themselves Jewish by ethnicity only. Roughly half of modern Israel describes themselves as secular, and one in five do not even believe in God.[79] Religious Judaism today is one of the only non-evangelical religions in the world. Although many religious Jews do believe that there are ways for people of non-Jewish descent to join the faith, very few are actively sharing their faith with others in hopes of bringing them into a right-standing relationship with God. Pew Research Center noted in 2015 that, "the share of the world's population that is Jewish – 0.2% – is expected to remain about the same in 2050 as it was in 2010."[80] Imagine how this grieves the heart of God! So many of His

---

[79] "Israel's Religiously Divided Society," *PewResearch.org*, March 8, 2016. https://www.pewresearch.org/religion/2016/03/08/israels-religiously-divided-society/.

[80] "Jews," *PewResearch.Org*, April 2, 2015. https://www.pewresearch.org/religion/2015/04/02/jews/.

chosen people do not know Him or call Him by name. They have thus far rejected the new covenant, but many have also neglected the old covenant.

JERUSALEM

All four of the gospel accounts record the story of Jesus entering Jerusalem as King. (Matt. 21:1-11; Mark 11:1-11; Luke 19:28-44; John 12:12-19). Matthew and John both highlighted how Jesus riding in on a donkey fulfilled one of Zechariah's prophesies (Matt. 21:1-5; John 12:14-15; Zech. 9:9). As He entered the city gates, the people shouted, "Save us, Son of David!" and they proclaimed words from the psalms, saying, "Blessed is he who comes in the name of the Lord" (Matt. 21:9; Mark 11:9; Ps 118:25-26). Both Luke and John even have the word king, as they said, "Blessed is the king of Israel" (John 12:13) and "Blessed is the king who comes in the name of the Lord" (Luke 19:38; Ps 118:26). John said that even Jesus' disciples did not understand any of this until after His crucifixion and resurrection (John 12:16). But Luke's gospel shares an interesting interaction that the other gospels do not have.

Upon hearing the shouts of praise and worship, the religious leaders told Jesus to rebuke His disciples for blasphemy (Luke 19:39). Jesus responded by saying, "If they keep quiet, the stones will cry out" (Luke 19:40). Was He alluding to the literal stones, saying that all of creation cries out His praises (Ps. 96:13)? Perhaps He was alluding to the Gentile descendants of Abraham, from where John the Baptist had said out of stones God could "raise up children for Abraham" (Matt. 3:9). Perhaps He was alluding to the stones of the devastated temple that would symbolize God's Spirit never again being contained in a temple built by man (Mark 13:1-2). Regardless of whether or not He was alluding to any or all of those concepts, He was telling the religious leaders that the praise and worship could not be stopped. They would continue to try to squelch the worshipers of Jesus, bought with His blood, but they would not succeed.

Luke then said that as they approached Jerusalem, Jesus saw the city and wept over it (Luke 19:41). For the Israelites of that time, Jerusalem would have automatically been associated with the temple. It always symbolized God's presence. Matthew records Him saying, "Jerusalem, Jerusalem, you who kill the prophets and stone those sent to you, how often I have longed to gather your children together, as a hen gathers her chicks under her wings, and you were not willing" (Matt. 23:37). The incarnate Presence of God was there, yet they still flocked to the empty temple. The depth of His pain for how far Israel had swayed from God is palpable. God's heart longs for Israel to return to the covenant. He longs to gather them into the loving relationship He had proposed at Mount Sinai. He has not given up on His beloved nor has He replaced her with another. He is the one waiting for her return to Him. This should be the prayer of the Church today.

The Mount of Olives is a small hill that overlooks the city of Jerusalem. The view is breathtaking today, as I am sure it was back then. Of course, the view has changed drastically in the last 2,000 years. Today, Jerusalem is surrounded by roads packed with cars and abuzz with tourists from all nations. Where the temple mount once stood, today is the gleaming golden dome of the Muslim's pride and joy, the Al Aqsa Mosque. Whether standing on the Mount of Olives today or in the time of Jesus, the path into the city would take you straight to the Golden Gate, sometimes called the Gate of Mercy. It "is the only eastern gate of the Temple Mount, and one of only two Gates of the Old City of Jerusalem that used to offer access into the city from the East side."[81]

Going from the Mount of Olives to the temple, which is what the Scripture shows was Jesus' path that day, He would have entered the city through that gate. Unfortunately, it is impossible to enter that gate today because it has been sealed shut since 1541, which is actually the most recent of several attempts to seal the gate shut. It was originally shut in 810 by the Muslims, opened in 1102 by the Crusaders, and closed again in 1187. The reason is because Jewish tradition said that the Messiah would enter though that gate and the Muslims were trying to prevent that from happening by closing it up. Unfortunately, their efforts were too little, too late, for what brick wall could ever stop the Messiah? Furthermore,

---

[81] "Golden Gate (Jerusalem)," *En.Wikipedia.org*, 2024, https://en.wikipedia.org/wiki/Golden_Gate_(Jerusalem).

the Messiah had already entered through that gate eight centuries before Islam even existed after He wept for the city that refused to be gathered back to the Lord.

Today, Jerusalem is without question the most important religious city in the world, with all three major world religions claiming it as central to their beliefs. As we have seen here, Jerusalem is the city of David, and its importance to the Jewish faith cannot be overstated. It is also the city where Jesus was crucified, buried, and raised from the dead, thus making it historically meaningful to Christians. Lastly, Muslims believe that their prophet Muhammad had a profound spiritual experience in Jerusalem, making it one of their three holiest cities and why the Al Aqsa Mosque stands in that location. Within the walls of Jerusalem today, there are the Jewish, Christian, Muslim, and Armenian quarters, with all groups claiming ownership rights over this beloved city.

Much of the city has been destroyed and rebuilt countless times. In places you can even see the levels of history, as one conquering nation built atop the ruins of the previous one. In the Jewish quarter, there is a remnant of the original temple wall that still stands. This portion of wall at the Temple Mount dates to the second temple period and is incredibly precious to the Jewish people. It is known as the Wailing Wall, and it is a reminder to the Jewish people of the time in their history where God's Presence resided among them. What is so complicated is that on the other side of the wall is the Temple Mount, which would have historically been the Holy of Holies where God's Presence literally resided. Today, however, that is the site of the Al Aqsa Mosque. Entry into that area is controlled by Israeli and Islamic law. For many Jews, they feel that the Western Wall is the closest to His Presence that they can get.

The Temple Mount where the mosque is located is central to Islamic belief, as well. According to one publication, "In the Quran, Al Aqsa and its surrounding area is described as 'blessed'. According to the Islamic worldview, the term 'blessed land' means a territory over which God has granted physical and spiritual bounties from which all creation can profit."⁸² Muslims do not believe the actual presence of God resided there because their theology does not allow for God's presence to reside among mankind, but the area does contain spiritual significance to them.

Jesus' words and actions showed He cared significantly less about the brick-and-mortar aspect of the city of Jerusalem than He did for her people. There is nothing in Scripture that indicates that His heart was grieved when He predicted the destruction of the temple as much as it grieved His heart to see the "sheep without a shepherd" (Matt. 9:35-38). He said to His disciples, "The harvest is plentiful but the workers are few. Ask the Lord of the harvest, therefore, to send out workers into his harvest field" (Matt. 9:37-38). The Jews were the sheep without a shepherd (Ez. 34), but so were the Gentiles who had not been led to the Lord by the nation of Israel. Jesus said, "I have other sheep that are not of this sheep pen. I must bring them also. They too will listen to my voice, and there shall be one flock and one shepherd" (John 10:16). He came and willingly laid down His life in the holy city of Jerusalem for the Jews *and* the Gentiles.

Why then is Jerusalem seemingly more significant to the Jews and the Muslims than it is for the Christians? There is a perceived holiness in Jerusalem that exists for Jews and Muslims that does not exist in the same way for Christians. For many Christian pilgrims who visit Jerusalem, they might certainly have a spiritual encounter and feel as if they are closer to God there. But the reality is that the Spirit of God no longer resides in any physical dwelling in Jerusalem. The Spirit of God is not contained in the ark of the covenant or the Holy of Holies or the Temple Mount. The Spirit of God now resides in the believer. So, if you as a believer go to Jerusalem and have a spiritual experience, it is not because the Spirit of God is more present there than back at your own home. You would have *carried* the Presence of God all the way from your home, on the airplane across the globe, to the streets of Jerusalem because as a Christian, you are the walking, talking, breathing Temple of God (1 Corin. 6:19).

If Jerusalem fell today, the Jews would grieve deeply the loss of their last

---

[82] "Al Aqsa Mosque: Why is it So Special in Islam?" *TRTWorld.com*, 2024, https://www.trtworld.com/magazine/al-aqsa-mosque-why-is-it-so-special-in-islam-12797653

connection to the temple and the Holy of Holies. The Muslims would grieve deeply the loss of their beloved Al Aqsa Mosque. The Christians would certainly grieve the loss of a significant piece of our history, but it would have no bearing on our *faith* because God's Spirit is not contained solely in Jerusalem. Furthermore, the promised land does not contain the strategic significance that it did pre-Jesus. People from all over the world do not need to go through the promised land to encounter the Presence of God in order to take that message back to their own people. People from all over the world who carry the Glory of God through the Holy Spirit become a miniature, mobile promised land.

Paul said to the believers in Ephesus that there was a time where the Gentiles were "excluded from citizenship in Israel and foreigners to the covenants of the promise" (Eph. 2:12), but that is no longer the case because of Jesus! Now, Paul says, "In Christ Jesus you who once were far away have been brought near" (Eph. 2:13). This whole passage of Scripture talks about the Jews and Gentiles being reconciled through Christ Jesus. Paul is not saying one has replaced the other, but rather, the Gentiles are "no longer foreigners and strangers, but fellow citizens with God's people … being built together to become a dwelling in which God lives by his Spirit" (Eph. 2:19, 22). Through Jesus, members of His Church are "heirs together with Israel" (Eph. 3:6). As a Christian, you have the honor and privilege of being blessed to be a blessing, using your blessings and your testimony to bless all peoples of the earth. As Paul said, Jesus "redeemed us in order that the blessing given to Abraham might come to the Gentiles through Christ Jesus, so that by faith we might receive the promise of the Spirit" (Gal. 3:14). The Abrahamic covenant is now inclusive of the Spirit-filled follower of Jesus.

THE CHURCH AND ISRAEL

The mission of Israel has been given also to the Church. The Church has not *replaced* Israel, for "there is no favoritism with him" (Eph. 6:9), but rather the Church has been given an equal assignment in Israel's original mission. The Church has been grafted into the lineage and purpose of Abraham and his descendants. This imagery of being grafted from Paul's letter to the church in Rome (Rom. 11) is a horticultural concept. With olive trees in particular, a branch can be taken from a newer tree and grafted it into an older tree. It involves cutting a slit or opening into the older tree and in a way, planting the new shoot into that part of the old tree. The older tree will take the branch as one of its own and eventually life will flow from the older root into the newer branch. They become one. The grafted branch does not replace the whole tree. In fact, a grafted branch without the older tree is useless! It is, as Jesus said, a branch apart from the vine that "can do nothing" (John 15:5-6). The Church, the body of believers, can do nothing apart from the rooted tree in which it is grafted, which is the Old Testament covenant.

Today many Christians have the incorrect assumption that the Old Testament is irrelevant history. I certainly hope at this point that you see the error in that thinking. Furthermore, many Christians view the faith as simply a means to end up in the desired destination of the afterlife. But the Christian faith is about so much more than where we go when we die. It is about the purpose for which we live. We have been grafted into a story that God has been writing since the beginning of time. Not only that, but God has given each of us a role to play in that story.

Jesus commissioned His followers to make disciples of all nations, a task that once complete would fulfill the Abrahamic covenant and bring representation around the heavenly throne from every nation, tribe, and tongue. When Jesus used the word "nation," the word did not necessarily correlate to geo-political nations. The word He used was "ethne" or "ethnos," and it corresponds more to ethno-linguistic groups. Strong's Concordance describes it as "a multitude of individuals of the same nature; a tribe; the human family; people group." The Joshua Project is a research initiative that seeks to identify how many unique "ethnos" there are in the world today and how many of them have a growing movement of Christ-followers within them. They seek "to answer the questions that result from the Great Commission's call to make disciples among every nation or people group."[83] According to their most recent data, there are 17,291 unique people groups or ethne in the world representing a global population of 8 billion people. Of those 8 billion, 3.4 billion are considered unreached by the gospel.

Unreached does not necessarily mean that nobody has reached out to them yet with the message of Jesus, although that is typically true. Unreached is about access to the gospel. They are considered unreached by Joshua Project if less than 2% of their population is composed of evangelical Christians. It is a people group that has not yet had the gospel of the kingdom proclaimed as a testimony (Matt. 24:14). It does not necessarily refer to lost people, non-Christians, or even post-Christian nations. It is a group of people, a tribe, a community, an ethnicity that does not have churches or Christians in their midst, Bibles available in their language, or any disciple-making movements among them. They have not yet been reconciled to Yahweh because they have not yet heard of Him. As Paul said in Romans 10:11-15, quoting Isaiah and Joel:

> As Scripture says, "Anyone who believes in him will never be put to shame" (Is. 28:16). For there is no difference between Jew and Gentile—the same Lord is Lord of all and richly blesses all who call on him, for, "Everyone who calls on the name of the Lord will be saved" (Joel 2:23). How, then, can they call on the one they have not believed in? And how can they believe in the one of whom they have not heard? And how can they hear without someone preaching to them? And how can anyone preach unless they are sent? As it is written: "How beautiful are the feet of those who bring good news!" (Is. 52:7).

Of the 17,291 unique people groups identified by the Joshua Project, 7,253 are considered unreached. That is 41.9% of the world's population. The only place in Scripture where Jesus says when the end will come indicates that it will not happen until all 17,291 people groups have had the gospel of the kingdom preached among them. Therefore, Jesus said, "Go and make disciples of *all ethne*" (Matt. 28:19, emphasis added).

---

[83] "Joshua Project, *JoshuaProject.net*, 2024, https://joshuaproject.net/about/details.

Reaching the nations was the purpose of old covenant, and Israel failed to bring the nations back to God; however, through Israel came the Savior of all, Jews and Gentiles. The Church has not replaced Israel as God's favorite or as the chosen one. But the task that was left incomplete under the old covenant has been issued to those under the new covenant. The Church is not the new Israel. This is not replacement theology. It is simply a new way of achieving the same thing. "See, the former things have taken place, and new things I declare; before they spring into being I announce them to you" (Is. 42:9). Israel can still walk in the covenant. But the covenant now includes the followers of Jesus Christ, empowered by the Holy Spirit. God said to Israel, whom He chose, "I will pour out my Spirit on your offspring, and my blessing on your descendants" (Is. 44:3). Joel prophesied the same thing, saying, "I will pour out my Spirit on all people" (Joel 2:28). That has been fulfilled since the day of Pentecost (Acts 2:17-21) and will continue until every nation, tribe, and tongue is represented around the holy throne of God (Rev. 7:9).

Conclusion

Israeli lives are sacred to the Lord. Palestinian lives are sacred to the Lord. Yahweh wants Israelis represented around the heavenly throne, worshiping the Lamb. Yahweh also wants Palestinians represented around the heavenly throne, worshiping the Lamb. Our job as the Church is to help Israeli Jews see the truth about Jesus and the new covenant as a continuation of their covenant. Our job is also to help Palestinian Muslims see the truth about Jesus and walk away from the lies that Islam teaches about Him. God does not call us to stand for or against any nation. We can stand for or against the *actions* of individuals and nations, but we cannot stand against any nation that God wants represented around the heavenly throne. Our job is to bring them to the throne. We cannot stand against any nation that Jesus bought with His blood, which is all of them. How can we bring Him the worship He is due if we are standing against a nation that does not yet have adequate representation around the throne? The heart of God grieves every Israeli life lost that had not yet had the opportunity to turn to Jesus. His heart grieves just as much for every Palestinian life lost that had yet to even hear the truth of Jesus.

Just after Joshua led the Israelites into the promised land, before they conquered the first city of Jericho, Joshua encountered "a commander of the army of the Lord" (Josh. 5:14). Many people believe that this was a theophany, or even a Christophany. A theophany is when God Himself appeared in human form, like when He wrestled with Jacob and changed his name to Israel. A Christophany is when Jesus appeared in human form before the incarnation, a pre-incarnate Christ. The grounds for this assumption is that when the commander introduced himself, "Joshua fell facedown to the ground in reverence" (Josh. 5:14). A commander in God's army who was not God Himself would not have received Joshua's worship. In fact, in Revelation, we see an example of this. An angel appeared before John and when John fell at the angel's feet in worship, the angel responded, "Don't do that! I am a fellow servant with you and with your brothers and sisters who hold to the testimony of Jesus. Worship God!" (Rev. 19:10) The commander did not rebuke Joshua's worship. In fact, he said, "Take off your sandals, for the place where you are standing is holy" (Josh. 5:15). Whether the commander of the army was a theophany or Christophany, He was clearly God in human form.

Before Joshua realized that, he asked the commander whose side he was on, saying, "Are you for us or for our enemies?" (Josh. 5:13). God had told Joshua that He would go with them into the land, that He would be their strength and their victory, and that no one would be able to stand against them (Josh. 1:5). He had said to Joshua, "I will be with you; I will never leave you nor forsake you … Be strong and courageous. Do not be afraid; do not be discouraged, for the Lord your God will be with you wherever you go" (Josh. 1:5, 9). God was seemingly for the Israelites. However, when Joshua asked the commander of the Lord's army, God in human form, whose side he was on, he said, "Neither" (Josh. 5:14). Neither? How could the Lord's commander not choose a side between the people of God and their enemies? If the commander was, in fact, God, all the more reason for Him to choose to side with His people. Yet, He said neither. He is for His purposes before He is for any one nation. Even His chosen nation.

The Western worldview pushes us to choose a side. There is no grey area in the Western worldview. If you are for one group, it must mean that you are against the other. Our justice-based mindset demands that in every conflict someone is given the title of "right" and therefore the other must be given the title of "wrong." Sometimes, though, both sides are right. Sometimes both sides are wrong. Always God is working towards His purposes and towards His will. Sometimes it is in collaboration with the actions of mankind, but often He is accomplishing His will despite our actions. And unfortunately, sometimes the will of Satan is accomplished while we live in this broken world overrun by sin. We "know that in all things God works for the good of those who love him" (Rom. 8:28) and regardless of the plans of men, "it is the Lord's purpose that prevails" (Prov. 19:21). As Christians, we can and should disagree with actions of one or both sides that stand against the will of God. However, as Christians, we cannot unconditionally take sides for or against an entire nation of people. We have to stand for both nations, for *all* nations, coming into the kingdom of God. To take any other stand is to stand against the entire message of the Old and New Testaments. It is to stand against everything that Jesus came for.

Appendix 1
End Times Prophecy

The big question remains whether or not modern-day Israel is a fulfillment, in part or in whole, of end times prophecy? Personally, I believe that many of the end times prophetic messages that are used to justify this opinion are taken out of context. Those are the ones that have been addressed in the context of this book. For two millennia, theologians and pastors have debated on what the end times will look like. To be honest, eschatology is personally one of my least favorite theological discussions; however, in an attempt not to leave the question unanswered, I will at least address it very briefly.

I do believe that God's hand was with His people when He rescued them from the atrocities of World War II and the Holocaust. I also believe that the Church failed at standing up against those atrocities. There were people in high-ranking positions within the Catholic and Protestant churches that knew what was happening and did nothing. In a quote attributed to many throughout history, "The only thing necessary for the triumph of evil is for good men to do nothing." In the face of pure evil, the powers-that-be in the Church did nothing.[84]

Yet, God heard the cries of His people, and He rescued a remnant and brought them from the ends of the earth to the land of their forefathers. This has under-

---

[84] For an example of this, read the response of Corrie Ten Boom's pastor in *The Hiding Place*

Appendix 1 - End Times Prophecy

standably brought up so many questions about end times prophecy. The Israelites were scattered from the land shortly after the time of Jesus when the temple was destroyed in 70 A.D. As we have seen, most of the prophecy about the Israelites coming back into the land has them united once again and under the authority of King Jesus. Therefore, the debate has raged on since 1944/1946 about whether or not their return to the land is the beginning of the end.

There is one time in particular where Jesus talked about the end times. In Matthew chapter twenty-four, His disciples asked Him "When will this happen, and what will be the sign of your coming and of the end of the age?" (Matt. 24:3). Jesus warned them about deceivers coming in His name, "wars and rumors of wars," nations and kingdoms rising against one another, "famines and earthquakes in various places," persecution of the believers, betrayal and hatred within the Church, and false prophets while wickedness increases, and love decreases (Matt. 24:4-12). For two millennia we have witnessed all of these things. None of these things are newer or more prolific now than they have been at any other point of history since Jesus.

Furthermore, these are all things outside of the control of the Church. Sure, we can pray against them, and there is power in that. We can seek peace where it is possible. However, these are circumstances that all result from living in a fallen world. Yet, there is one sign that is well within the control of the Church. Of all the signs of the end times that Jesus lists in Matthew chapter twenty-four, there is one that is dependent on the actions of the Church. In verse fourteen, which we have already discussed, is the only sign that is contingent on the actions of the body of believers: "This gospel of the kingdom will be preached in the whole world as a testimony to all nations." After that has happened, the end will come.

I will not say that Israel returning to the land of her forefathers cannot be like the budding of the fig tree (Matt. 24:32). However, Jesus followed that analogy with the statement, "Truly I tell you, this generation will certainly not pass away until all these things have happened" (Matt. 24:34). What do we make of that? The generation He spoke to has passed away, as have many others since then. All of the signs He mentioned in verses four through twelve have been seen, and yet He has not returned. I would argue that it is because the one sign contingent on the actions of the Church has not yet been fulfilled. The gospel of the kingdom has not yet been preached as a testimony to all nations.

How must we approach eschatology and the modern-day nation of Israel? I would argue that we take to heart Jesus' words to the apostles in Acts chapter one. Before He ascended, the disciples asked Him if He was now going to "restore the kingdom of Israel" (Acts 1:6). They were still waiting on the restoration of a physical kingdom, instead of the spiritual kingdom that Jesus actually came to usher in. Jesus' response to them is so telling. He said, "It is not for you to know the times or dates the Father has set by his own authority" (Acts 1:7). To His closest followers, He said it is not for you to know. Why? He tells them in the very next verse. It is not for you to know because it is not your concern. The concern of the Church should be much more about fulfilling the task given to us than speculating on how and when He will return!

When He said to them, "It is not for you to know the times or dates" (Acts 1:7), He then said, "But (rather, instead of the question you are asking) you will receive power from the Holy Spirit in order to fulfill the task you have been given, which is taking the gospel of the kingdom to the ends of the earth!" (Acts 1:8, paraphrase mine) That is twice now that when asked about end times, He redirected His followers to the task they had been given. In other words, stop worrying about when the end will come, what it will look like, and how the kingdom will be restored. Just focus on the task at hand! Just focus on doing the work you have been commissioned to do!

Nobody can definitively say whether or not modern-day Israel is the partial or final fulfillment of prophecy, other than Jesus. Nobody can say definitely if this is the beginning of end times, other than the Father who determines that. Nobody can say whether or not modern-day Israel will be allowed to stay in the land indefinitely if they refuse to walk in the covenant, as their ancestors did time and time again. The point is, as the body of believers, we too must stop overemphasizing when and how the end will come at the expense of how Jesus said it will come. We must stay focused on the task at hand, neither looking to the left nor the right. George Eldon Ladd said, "He alone will know when that goal is fulfilled. But I do not need to know. I know only one thing: Christ has not yet returned; therefore, the task is not yet done. When it is done, Christ will come. Our responsibility is not to insist on defining the terms; *our responsibility is to complete the task*. So long as Christ does not return, our work is undone. Let us get busy and complete our mission."[85] Arguing eschatology does not get the gospel to the ends of the earth. Only obedience to the task will do that.

---

[85] Ladd, "The Gospel of the Kingdom," 94.

Acknowledgments

This project is over seven years in the making. I thank God that He was patient with how many times I cried out my hesitations and deficiencies while simultaneously begging Him not to assign it to someone else. I am forever grateful that You, God, have preserved Your Word for all of history to know You. Thank you, Abba, for trusting me with this project.

As for my earthly expressions of gratitude, first and foremost I have to thank my amazing husband, Parker. Thank you for the holy wrestling you did with me and with Abba as we navigated difficult conversations with love and truth and grace. Thank you for believing in me, for supporting me, and for always being my #1 fan and biggest cheerleader. Thanks for working extra hard to make money to give to mommy so that she could go to school and write books. You're my favorite, forever and always, and I love you.

Thank you to my children ME, LP, and JV who unknowingly supported me through this. You sacrificed alongside me as you shared your mommy's time. I recognize the sacrifice it can have on kids when mom is called to work in ministry, especially missions, but you have always shown grace and love. I pray that witnessing our sacrificial obedience impacts you all in the best way as you seek your own paths with Abba.

Acknowledgments

Thank you, Corrie, for being the first to read my manuscript, even knowing that you would not agree with all that I believe. Your grace, your friendship, and your feedback is precious to me.

Thank you, Chesed, for allowing me to force my friendship upon you. Your feedback was incredibly valuable and so encouraging. Reading your comments felt like having the best conversation with an old friend over a cup of tea. And your artwork now graces the cover of one of my most important works. Thank you.

Thank you, David Gineris, for your help navigating the publishing and printing world, and for cheering me on. Thank you, Eric Casaubon, for being such a great guide and coach through this process. I pray that God meets you on your journey in beautiful and unexpected ways. Thank you, Christie Carey, for being a great friend and coworker, and for using your God-given talents to help share this message.

Thank you to my Brazilian bishop, João Carlos Lopes and his wife, my mentor, Audir. Our conversations on our road trip in Brazil gave me insight, encouragement, and confidence which are valuable beyond what words can express. Thank you for translating my first book and thank you (in advance!) for translating this one!

To Fuad for the encouragement and support, I hope you feel seen and honored. To Steph for the emotional support, always. To Heather Cobb who kept pointing me back to Jesus and obedience. To the countless other who have encouraged and cheered me on through this process, thank you. To my dad for the genetic gift of confidence bordering arrogance. To David Horn for obediently supporting me in a time where I felt very alone in this. And of course, to my mama, Megan. Thanks for literally always believing in me and instilling in me the belief that I can do anything I set my mind to. I'm sorry for the ways that must have driven you crazy when I was a child.

Bibliography

Abarim Publications website, "Eliezer meaning." November 22, 2023. https://www.abarim-publications.com/Meaning/Eliezer.html

Behind the Name website, "Eliezer." June 9, 2023. https://www.behindthename.com/name/eliezer;

Bird, Michael F., ed. *Four Views on the Apostle Paul.* Grand Rapids, MI: Zondervan, 2012.

Chisholm, Robert B. *Handbook on the Prophets.* Grand Rapids, MI: Baker Academic, 2009.

Comer, John Mark. *God has a Name.* Grand Rapids, MI: Zondervan, 2017.

Elwell, Walter A., and Robert W. Yarbrough. *Encountering the New Testament: A Historical and Theological Survey.* 3rd ed. Grand Rapids, MI: Baker Academic, 2013.

Evans, Craig A. *Luke.* Grand Rapids, MI: Baker Publishing Group, 2011.

Forrest, Benjamin, and Chet Roden. *Biblical Leadership: Theology for the Everyday Leader.* Grand Rapids, MI: Kregel Academic, 2017.

Goerner, H. Cornell. "Jesus and the Gentiles." In *Perspectives on the World Christian Movement: A Reader*, 112–17. Pasadena, CA: William Carey Library, 2009.

Green, Yosef. "The Reign of King Solomon." *The Jewish Bible Quarterly.* 42, no. 3 (2014): 151–158.

Hamilton, Victor P. *Handbook on the Historical Books: Joshua, Judges, Ruth, Samuel, Kings, Chronicles, Ezra-Nehemiah, Esther.* Grand Rapids, MI: Baker Academic, 2001.

Hamilton, Victor P. *Handbook on the Pentateuch: Genesis, Exodus, Leviticus, Numbers, Deuteronomy.* Grand Rapids, MI: Baker Academic, 2015.

Howell, Don N., Jr. *Servants of the Servant: A Biblical Theology of Leadership.* Eugene, OR: Wipf & Stock Publishers, 2003.

Joshua Project website, "About Joshua Project." 2023. https://joshuaproject.net/about/details

Ladd, George Eldon. "The Gospel of the Kingdom." In *Perspectives on the World Christian Movement: A Reader*, 83-95. Pasadena, CA: William Carey Library, 2009.

Moore, Russell. *Adopted for Life.* Wheaton, IL: Crossway, 2015.

Pew Research Center website, "Israel's Religiously Divided Society." March 8, 2016. https://www.pewresearch.org/religion/2016/03/08/israels-religiously-divided-society/

Pew Research Center website, "Jews." April 2, 2015. https://www.pewresearch.org/religion/2015/04/02/jews/

Rubin, Jordan S. *The Maker's Diet.* Shippensburg, PA: Destiny Image Publishers, 2005.

Stein, Robert H. *Luke.* Vol. 24, *The New American Commentary,* edited by David S. Dockery, et al. Nashville, TN: B&H Publishing Group, 1992.

Stott, John R. W. "The Living God is a Missionary God." In *Perspectives on the World Christian Movement: A Reader*, 3-9. Pasadena, CA: William Carey Library, 2009.

TRT World website, "Al Aqsa Mosque: Why is it So Special in Islam?" March 2023. https://www.trtworld.com/magazine/al-aqsa-mosque-why-is-it-so-special-in-islam-12797653

Voyakin, Dmitry. UNESCO Website. "The Great Silk Road." https://en.unesco.org/silkroad/knowledge-bank/great-silk-road#:~:text=The%20Great%20Silk%20Road%20is,the%20West%20and%20the%20East.

W, Jackson. *Reading Romans with Eastern Eyes*. Downers Grove, IL: InterVarsity Press, 2019.

Wikipedia website, "Golden Gate (Jerusalem)." October 29, 2023. https://en.wikipedia.org/wiki/Golden_Gate_(Jerusalem)

Winter, Ralph. "The 'First Chapter' of the Bible: Genesis 12–50." WCF Lecture, around 1995, as World Christian Foundations curriculum was being developed.

Woodhouse, John. *1 Kings: Power, Politics, and the Hope of the World*. Wheaton, IL: Crossway, 2018.

Wright, N.T. *The New Testament in its World*. Great Britain: Society for Promoting Christian Knowledge, 2019.

Scripture Index

GENESIS
1:1, 26-28; *6*
1:28; *9, 11, 33, 119*
1:31; *7*
2:16, 17, 18; *7*
3; *39*
3:3, 5, 6, 10, 12; *7*
3:8; *7, 121*
3:15; *101, 120*
3:16-19, 21, 22; *8*
4:6-8; *9*
4:10; *9, 132*
4:23; *33*
5:3, 24; *9*
6:3, 9, 18; *9*
7:11; *9*
8:16-17; *10*
9:1, 7; 10, *11*
9:3, 4-5, 6; *10*
9:4; *132*
9:20-25; *14*
10; *10*
11:4; *10-11*
11:9; *11*
11:22-23; *12*
11:27-32; *13*
11:30; *14*
12; *12*
12:1; *13, 37*
12:2-3; *12, 13, 14, 21, 26, 29, 39, 96, 112, 131*
12:4; *13, 14*
12:7; *15*
13:15-16; *15, 18*
14; *50*
15; *134*
15:2-3, 4, 8; *15*
15:5; *15, 18*
15:6; *15, 131*
15:9-10, 12, 17; *16*
15:13, 16; *17, 29, 50*
15:18; *16, 17, 37, 86*
15:18-21; *70*
15:19-20; *48*
16:2, 4-6, 7-9, 10, 11, 13; *18*
17:2, 4; *18*
17:5-8, 10-11; *19*
17:15-16, 17, 18, 19-21, 23-27; *20*
17:20; *20, 25*
18:10-15, 17-19; *21*
18:12; *22*
18:16-19:38; *50*
19:30-38; *101*
21:6, 8-9, 10, 11, 12-13; *22*
21:17-18, 20; *23*
22:5, 8, 9-10; *23*

22:16-18; *23-24*
24:2-4, 6-8, 10-59, 60; *24*
25:5; *24*
25:7-10, 12-18, 20-21, 27-34; *25*
25:23; *25, 28*
26:1-3, 3-5; *25*
26:2-3; *29*
26:24; *25-26*
27:1-27, 29; *26*
28:1-2, 3-4, 10-15; *26*
28:3; *26, 28*
28:13-14; *26-27, 35*
29; *27*
30; *27*
31:3; *27, 29*
32:22-30, 26, 28; *27*
35:11-12; *28*
35:22; *29*
37:3, 4-11; *28*
37:21-22, 21-28; *29*
38; *101*
41:41-43, 46-49; *29*
46:3-4; *29*

EXODUS
1:6-7, 9-10, 15-22; *30*
2:1; *44*
2:11-15; *31*
3:6, 10, 11, 12; *31*
3:8; *31, 37*
4:1, 10, 13; *31*
4:22-23; *32, 35, 103*
6:2-4, 7-8; *32*
7:14-24; *32*
7:16; *33*
8:1, 10, 20, 22; *33*
8:1-15, 16-19; *32*
9:1, 13, 14, 29; *33*
9:13-35; *32*
9:13-16; *32-33*
10:2, 3; *33*
11:9; *33*
12:12; *32*
12:38; *34*
13:2, 12; *122*
14:4, 17-18, 31; *34*
15:13; *36*
15:26; *45*
18:1, 9, 10, 11-12; *34*
19:4-6; *36, 39, 69*
19:5-6; *75, 83, 89, 95, 118, 134*
19:7-8, 10-15, 16; *39*
19:10-11; *121*
20:3, 4-7, 6, 8-11, 12; *40*
20:3-6; *46-47*
20:5-6; *41*
20:7; *46*
23:25-26; *40*
23:30; *50*
23:32-33; *50*
24:8; *123*
28:1; *44*
32:1-4, 9-10, 13, 20; *41*
33:1, 3, 20; *42*
33:15-16; 40-41, *135*
34:5-7; *50*
34:6; *46, 47*
34:10; *41*
39:43; *42*
40:12-15; *121*
40:34; *42*
40:36-38; *43*

LEVITICUS
19:18; *40, 50*
19:33-34; *50*
21:6; *24*
22:32; *24*
26:3-5, 5-8, 9-12, 16, 17, 18, 20; *46*
26:44; *47*

NUMBERS
5:11-31; *41*
13:1, 28; *47*
13:6, 8; *48*
14:21-23; *48*
14:24; *49*
20:12; *49*
32:12; *48*

DEUTERONOMY
1:8; *50, 96*
2:2; *49*
4:1, 40; *51*
4:5-8; *38-39, 51*
4:6; *76*
4:9; *51*

Scripture Index

4:32-35; *52*
5:33; *51*
6:3, 18, 24-25; *51*
6:4-9; *51*
6:5; *40*
6:8; *89*
7:4; *51*
7:6; *52, 135*
9:5-6; *50*
10:12-13; *52*
11:22; *52*
17:14-15; *65*
17:16, 17; *75*
18:14, 15-20; *59*
23:3; *101*
26:18-19; *52*
28:1-14, 15-68, 64-66; *53*
30:1-5; *53, 136*
30:19-20; *53*
31:16; *53*
32:10; *130*
32:21, 43; *54*

JOSHUA

1:5, 9; *149*
1:6, 7, 9; *54*
2; *101*
2:9-11; *35*
4:24; *54*
5:13, 15; *149*
5:14; *148, 149*
6:21; *54*
8:22-23, 24, 27; *57*
10:1-15; *55*
14:6, 14; *48*
18:1; *57*
19:1; *57*
21:25; *57*
23 – 24; *55*
24:15, 16-18, 19-20, 21, 22; *55*

JUDGES

1:27-36; *56*
2:1-3, 10, 11-15, 16-17, 19, 22; *56*
6 – 7; *56*
8:28; *56*

RUTH

1; *101*
4:17-22; *101-102*

1 SAMUEL

2:26, 12-25, 27-36; *63*
3:1; *63*
5:4; *63*
6; *64*
6:1; *63*
8:5, 7-8, 9-18, 19-20; *64*
8:22; *68*
9:1; *65*
10:1, 10; *65*
12:13-15, 20-22; *65-66*
13:10, 13-14; *66*
15:26; *66*
16:1; *68, 85*
16:7, 13; *66*
17:12-19, 26, 45-46; *67*
18:16; *68*
26:9-11; *67*
26:23; *68*

2 SAMUEL

5:4, 6-10, 12; *69*
6:16-22; *66*
7:9, 12, 13, 15-16; *69*
7:16; *134*
7:18-19, 25-26; *70*
11; *102*
12:10-12, 13-17; *71*

1 KINGS

2:46; *74*
3:1-3; *74*
3:5, 6, 7-9, 10-13; *72*
4:26; *75*
4:29-34; *72*
5:7; *73*
6:38; *73*
8:41-43; *73, 115*
8:59-61; *73*
9:5; *73, 134*
9:6-7; *73*
9:14, 28; *75*
10:1-5, 6-9, 24; *74*
10:2, 10, 26-28; *75*
11:1-5, 14-27; *75*
11:3-4, 9, 11-13; *76*
17:7-24; *113*

2 KINGS
5:1-15; *113*
5:1, 15; *78*
14:25; *92*
17:14, 18-23; *78-79*

1 CHRONICLES
15:14; *121*
16:8-31; *68-69*
17:8, 11, 12, 14; *69*
22; *121*
22:8; *71*
22:9-10; *71-72*
28 – 29; *121*
29:5; *121*

2 CHRONICLES
5:11; *121*
7:14; *78*
7:19-21; *77*
10:19; *77*
36:15-17, 19-20; *79*

EZRA
6; *96*

NEHEMIAH
9:30-31, 36-37; *96*

PSALMS
22; *106-108*
48:9; *122*
69:9; *122*
78:2; *106*
84:1; *122*
96; *68-69*
96:13; *140*
103:19; *116*
105; *68-69*
118:22; *138*
118:25-26; *140*
145:11; *116*

PROVERBS
3:12; *136*
19:21; *149*

ECCLESIASTES
1:12-18; *76*
12:13; *76*

ISAIAH
1:2-3, 5, 7, 13; *93*
2:3; *75*
5:13, 24, 25, 26; *93*
6:9, 10; *106*
7:13, 14; *94, 101*
9:1-2; *105*
9:6; *95, 101*
9:6-7; *95-96*
26:18; *93*
28:16; *146*
29:13; *105*
40:3, 5; *105, 120*
41:8-10, 13-14; *94*
42:1; *122*
42:4; *106*
42:6; 38, *103*
42:6-7; *93*
42:8; *41*
42:8-9; *94, 147*
43:18-19; *94, 120*
44:3; *147*
44:21-22; *95*
45:22-23; *94*
47:13; *103*
48:9-11; *46*
48:11; *24*
49:5; *75*
49:6; *69, 75, 94*
49:22; *95, 139*
49:26; *94-95*
52:7; *102, 146*
52:15; *123, 138*
53:3; *138*
53:4; *105*
56:3-8; *95*
56:7; *114-115*
58:6; *112-113*
61:1-2; *112-113*
61:4-6, 8-9; *95*
66:18; *95*
66:19-20; *134*

JEREMIAH
2:3, 11, 13; *88*
3:19, 20; *88*
4:1-2, 18; *88*
5:17; *88*

7:11; *115*
11:1-4, 8, 10, 14; *139*
23:1-2, 3; *88*
23:5-6; *88, 139*
25; *96*
31:31; *89*
31:32, 33-34; *139*
33:14-16; *88*
33:22; *88-89*
50:2; *136*
50:4-5; *137*

LAMENTATIONS
4:2; *124*

EZEKIEL
3:5-7; *91*
4; *90*
5:5; *38*
11:19; *89*
16:3, 5; *130*
34; *102, 143*
34:10, 11, 17, 23; *91*
36:21-23; *90*
36:23; *24*
36:24-28; *137*
36:26-27; *89, 138*
36:28; *138*
37:15-28; *91, 138*
37:25-26, 28; *91*
38:23; *91*

DANIEL
3:16-18, 25, 27, 28-29; *80*
6:12-14, 22, 25-27; *81, 96*

HOSEA
1:2-9; *82*
6:6; *83*
9:17; *83*
11:1-2; *82, 103*
14; *83*

JOEL
2:23; *146*
2:28-29; *87, 147*
2:32; *87*
3:18; *87*

AMOS
3:2; *83*

JONAH
2:9; *92*
3:5; *92*
4:1; *92*

MICAH
2:6-7, 8-9, 10, 11; *83-84*
4:1-3; *84*
5:2-4; *84-85, 102*

ZECHARIAH
2:10-13; *85*
3:1-13; *85*
3:4, 6-7, 8, 9; *86*
8:13; *86*
9:9-10; *86, 140*
9:13; *86*
10:4; *86*
11:14; *86*
12:4, 7-9, 10-14; *87*
13:1; *87*

MALACHI
3:1; *105*

MATTHEW
1:1-16, 20-21; *101*
1:1-17; *111-112*
1:18-19; *133*
1:23; *94*
2:1-8, 12-15, 23; *103*
2:6; *85*
3:1-3; *94*
3:1-12; *105*
3:9; *140*
3:16; *122*
4:13, 14-16; *105*
4:18-22; *109*
5:14-16; *38*
5:17; *104*
6:10; *117*
8:4; *110*
8:17; *105*
9:9-13; *109*
9:15; *133*

9:18-26, 27-30; *110*
9:35-38; *143*
10:5-8; *109, 111*
10:6; *3, 86*
10:7; *117*
11:1-15; *105*
12:21; *106*
13:14, 35; *106*
15:2, 3, 6, 7-9; *105*
15:21-28; *86*
15:23, 26, 27, 28; *110*
15:24; *109*
21:1-11; *140*
21:6-11; *86*
21:13; *95*
22:34-40; *104*
22:36-40; *40*
23:37; *141*
24:1-2; *122*
24:3, 4-12; *152*
24:14; *5, 115, 119, 146, 152*
24:32, 34; *152*
25:31-46; *91*
26:26-28; *132, 134*
27:39, 46; *106*
27:27, 31, 43, 60; *107*
27:35; *108*
28:18-19; *108-109, 119, 146*

MARK
1:1-8; *105*
1:3; *120*
2:20; *133*
3:14; *109*
7:27; *110*
9:1; *121*
11:1-11; *140*
11:9; *95*
12:10; *138*
13:1-2; *122, 140*
14:22-25; *134*
15:20, 46; *107*
15:24, 29-32; *108*
15:29, 34; *106*
16:15-16; *120*

LUKE
1:29; *86*
1:30-33; *101, 129*
1:35; *101*
1:72-73; *112*
2:1-4; *102*
2:8-11; *102*
2:5,10, 11, 22; *102*
2:22-40, 41-52; *104*
2:22-23, 30-32; *122*
2:26; *102-103*
2:29-32; *103*
2:52; *63*
3:1-2, 1-20; *105*
3:6; *105*
3:8; *112*
3:23-37; *12, 102*
4; *93*

4:18-19, 22, 25-27, 28-30; *113*
5:17-26; *112*
5:35; *133*
7:1-10; *114*
7:11-17, 36-50; *112*
8; *114*
8:1-3; *112*
10:1-2; *111*
10:25-37; *114*
10:38-42; *112*
11:15, 17; *114*
11:29-32; *114*
13:35-43; *112*
14:15-24; *116-117*
16:19-31; *112*
17:18; *114*
17:20-21; *117*
18:1-8, 15-17, 35-43; *112*
19:28-44; *140*
19:46; *95, 115*
21:1-4; *112*
22:14-20; *134*
23:33, 53-54; *107*
23:34, 35; *108*
24:45-47; *118*
24:47; *120*

JOHN
1:1-5, 9, 14; *100*
1:18; *120*
1:19-28; *105*

Scripture Index

2:17; *122*
2:19-21; *122*
3:16-18; *5, 120, 131*
7:38; *87*
8:56; *127*
10:1-21; *91*
10:16; *143*
12:12-19; *140*
14:2; *129*
14:15-26; *89*
14:26; *123, 138*
15:5-6; *145*
16:7; *123*
16:13; *138*
16:13-15; *5, 89, 123*
17:1-5; *108*
17:5; *85*
17:18; *120*
19:34; *87, 107*
19:18, 38, 39-42; *107*
19:24; *108*

ACTS
1:6; *120, 153*
1:7; *153*
1:8; *86, 120, 123, 153*
2:17-21; *147*
2:21; *87*
8:1-3; *125*
9; *125*
13:6; *125*
21:23-26; *126*

ROMANS
4:1, 3, 6, 16; *131*
8:15-16; *130*
8:17; *131*
8:28; *149*
9:2-4; *126, 130*
9:6-8, 23-24; *128*
10:11-15; *146*
10:13; *87*
11; *145*
11:1, 11; *128*
11:25, 28; *139*
14:11; *94*

1 CORINTHIANS
6:19; *124, 143*

2 CORINTHIANS
4:7; *124*

GALATIANS
3:7-8; *126-127*
3:14; *127, 144*
3:26, 28-29; *127*

EPHESIANS
2:12-13; *128, 144*
2:14-18; *129*
2:19, 20-22; *129, 144*
3:6; *129, 144*
6:9; *144*

PHILIPPIANS
3:5-6; *126*

1 THESSALONIANS
3:13; *75*

2 THESSALONIANS
1:11; *4*

HEBREWS
4:12; *5*
8; *89*
9:18, 20, 21-22; *123*
9:28; *86*
10; *89*
10:19; *124*
11:7; *9*
12:6, 11; *136*

1 PETER
2:9-10; *89, 118*
2:24; *86*

1 JOHN
2:2; *86*
3:5; *86*

REVELATION
5:5-8; *134*
5:9; *5*
5:9-10; *134*
7:9; *147*
19:10; *149*

167 Chosen

About the Author

Nicole is a passionate advocate for the unreached and a lover of the word of God. She loves teaching and writing about God's big story and His global purposes. Her personal mission statement is to educate, equip, and empower members of the American church to understand the Great Commission and find their unique role in it. She has a BBA in International Business and a MA in Global Studies. She is currently pursuing a graduate level certificate in biblical Greek. She is an active Perspectives instructor, having taught at over 50 classes. She has spoken at multiple missions conferences and churches, both nationally and internationally. Her first published book is called *For God So Loved: A Seven Part Study on God's Heart for the World*. This Bible study helps readers understand God's heart for the nations and the biblical basis for missions. It has been translated into Portuguese and is currently being translated into Urdu. She also leads the missions effort at her church. Her love of travel and Jesus has brought her to over 30 different countries and counting. But her favorite role of all is full-time wife and mom to three children. When she's not writing or studying, she loves to travel, cook and eat good food, and snuggle on the couch with her family.

For more information or to book her for speaking, go to www.NicoleParksWrites.com. You can also follow her on Instagram.

Also by Nicole Parks

FOR GOD
— SO —
LOVED

A SEVEN PART STUDY ON GOD'S HEART FOR THE WORLD

The most often quoted verse in the entire Bible is John 3:16: "For God so loved the world that He gave His one and only Son…" It epitomizes the unconditional, sacrificial, grace-based loved of God. However, this love that God has for the world is not confined to this one verse. The message of John 3:16 is a thread woven intricately throughout the entire Bible, from Genesis to Revelation. God's love for the world is the story that ties all of the stories together.

In this study, you'll gain a better understanding of the Bible as a whole. You'll see the autobiography God has been writing since the beginning of time through the familiar stories, the obscure stories, and even your own story. Regardless of where you are in your faith, this study will help deepen your understanding of the Bible, God's purposes, and most of all, His love.

Author Nicole Parks is passionate about the unreached, mobilization, and helping Christians understand the truth about God's heart for the nations. She loves helping people understand the Bible in a way that ignites a passion within them to dive deep into the Word.

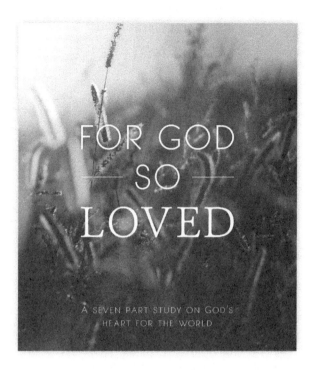

FEATURES

- Seven lessons each with 3 subsections
- An easy-to-understand overview of the entire Bible with 300+ scripture references
- Full color and beautifully illustrated
- Discussion/reflection questions after each subsection
- Deeper study questions after each lesson
- Leader guide and 'next step' suggestions
- Perfect for group or individual Bible study

Also available in Portuguese and coming soon in Urdu.

Available at www.NicoleParksWrites.com or Amazon